a passion for
Preserves

Frederica Langeland
Photography by Bill Milne

FRIEDMAN/FAIRFAX
PUBLISHERS

A FRIEDMAN/FAIRFAX BOOK

Library of Congress Cataloging in Publication Data

Langeland, Frederica.
    A passion for preserves : jams, jellies, marmalades, conserves,
    butters / Frederica Langeland.
          p.   cm.
    Includes index.
    ISBN 1-56799-533-0 (hc)
    1. Fruit—Preservation. 2. Canning and preserving.   I. Title.
TX612.F7L36   1997
641.4'2—dc21   97-13132

Editor: Nathaniel Marunas
Designer: Andrea Karman
Photography Editor: Christopher C. Bain
Production Director: Karen Matsu Greenberg

Color separations by Colourscan Pte Co Ltd.
Printed in Singapore by KHL Printing Co Pte Ltd.

1 3 5 7 9 10 8 6 4 2

For bulk purchases and special sales, please contact:
Friedman/Fairfax Publishers
Attention: Sales Department
15 West 26th Street
New York, New York 10010
212/685-6610 FAX 212/685-1307

Visit our website:
http://www.metrobooks.com

To Mim Chidsey,
who taught me to persevere.

Contents

Foreword

In Saint Tropez there is a small shop called *la Maison de la Confiture*, "the House of Jams." The owners of the shop make their own preserves in small, nonindustrial batches. The labels are handwritten, and beautiful gift boxes, covered with multicolored, pinked strips of gingham, may be purchased. The jars in these boxes are covered with pinked squares of the same fabric, tied down with a bit of white ribbon. The presentation is simple and quite stunning, but not enough so to prevent one from opening the jars and savoring the contents.

Some of the products from the House of Jams are straightforward, while some are made of unheard-of ingredients in exotic, undreamed-of combinations. The shop boasts four hundred jams, including a milk jam, which, the management assures one, is *à se rouler par terre*, "to die for."

This is all a far cry from the drearily familiar ten flavors of jam on your supermarket shelf, produced by three or four companies and full of commercial preservatives and other ingredients needed to guarantee consistent results in a mass-market product.

This book is not simply about making "gourmet" preserves; it is also about returning ordinary jam-making to the realm of possibility. And, once you have made strawberry jam, where everyone likes to start, why not add a liqueur, or peaches, or rhubarb, or your favorite spices? My hope is to be able to assist in this broadening process and in bringing no-fear jam-making back to your kitchen.

I first attempted making jam in Africa, where my husband and I had been living for several years. There in a market one fine day, amid lush piles of pineapples, mangoes, papayas, oranges—all very ho-hum commodities in that climate— were flats of strawberries. The succulent little gems were the result of a government effort at agricultural diversification, and what a success they were! To me, at least, they were irresistible. I took them home in huge, unreasonable quantities and set about "putting them up." It was not a happy beginning. The recipe was no problem, nor was the equipment— but my lack of experience combined with the great quantities involved very nearly defeated me. Perseverance did pay off on that occasion, and in succeeding years, at other addresses, I discovered that almost any fruit and many vegetables could be transformed into luscious spreads to enhance almost any meal.

On one hand, it is regrettable that our increased access to year-round produce has led to a standardization in what is available: the varieties of fruits and vegetables that ship better and last longer are what you usually find at the local market. On the other hand, while commercially regulated examples of produce abound at the sacrifice of more flavorful varieties, the advance of shipping technology also means that you have much wider access to exotic items from around the world. Those familiar bins and shelves can now provide you with a wildly diversified preserve cupboard.

MARGARITA PEARS (PAGE 124)

The Basics

Equipment

Although there is a certain amount of equipment necessary for preserving, most of it is fairly standard in any kitchen. The following is a list of things without which it is perilous to embark on a jam or jelly adventure.

KITCHEN SCALES
When dealing with solids, weight is a far more accurate measure than volume, which varies according to the food involved, the size of the chunks, etc.

LARGE POT WITH A HEAVY SOLID BOTTOM
Stainless steel and enameled cast iron are both excellent. Your pot should be large enough to hold four times the amount of fruit and sugar in any given batch, particularly if you will be using commercial pectins.

LARGE KETTLE OR CANNER
This is for sterilizing jars and lids. You might want to purchase a model equipped with a rack to accommodate boiling water bath processing.

KNIVES
A large one for chopping, and a good paring knife are recommended. In addition, a food processor, blender, food mill, or old-fashioned grinder, alone or in combination, will be a great labor saver.

COLANDER

JELLY BAG AND RACK
Your hardware store can supply you with these items, to use in straining cooked fruits. If they are not available, lining a colander with unbleached muslin or sheeting will achieve the same result. Cheesecloth is not a good substitute, being too loosely woven and not very strong. The rack is a long-legged chrome affair with little feet that perch on the rim of the bowl or pot. If you have a supply of bags but no rack, a bag may be tied between the legs of an upended kitchen stool with the bowl underneath. This is somewhat awkward but lends a fine pioneering atmosphere to the proceedings.

TIMER

SMALL UTENSILS
Measuring cups and spoons, long-handled wooden spoons, slotted spoon for skimming, tongs, widemouthed funnel (handy but not essential), non-metallic spatula for removing air bubbles from filled jars.

RACKS
These may be used for cooling hot jars. I find these tippy and prefer to use kitchen towels or, better yet, newspapers. Whatever you use, it is essential to set hot jars to cool on something other than cold tile, to avoid cracking.

JARS
The easiest to use are the standard jars available in various sizes at your hardware or grocery store. They are made of tempered glass meant to withstand the temperatures and pressures of the preserving process. The lids consist of three parts: metal disks coated on the inside, rubber sealing rings, and metal bands, which are reusable. The disks are not reusable, except in conjunction with paraffin, which then guarantees the seal and protects the preserves from damaged lid surfaces.

Perhaps, like me, you are an inveterate saver of jars. Those lovely little Italian condiment jars...French mustard pots...commercial jelly jars of all shapes and sizes...use them, too, but be aware that you must seal them with paraffin.

Do not attempt to use *any* jar that is cracked, chipped or damaged in any way. Damaged jars can result in spoilage or breakage.

PARAFFIN

This is not necessary except when you are reusing nonstandard jars or disks, as mentioned above. You will find it at the grocery store on the same shelf as jam jars. Melt paraffin in a small saucepan in hot water, not directly over the burner. Not only is paraffin highly flammable, if it is melted at too high a temperature it tends to shrink from the sides of the jar as it solidifies. It can also crack your jars if it is applied too hot. Keep any leftover paraffin in its saucepan, cover it, and store it like this for the next time you make jam. Do not attempt to wash and reuse paraffin from last year's jam jars. I've tried it. It leads to spoilage and other miseries.

THE KITCHEN STOVE

I will not recommend that you rush out and buy a new stove, but know the one you have. If it is a gas or an electric-coil model you have good control over the heat; if, on the other hand, you are dealing with a solid-plate electric model, you will need to take great care to avoid scorches.

PATIENCE

This is needed in great quantities.

Methods and Materials

Be methodical, to save your sanity. Before beginning any preserving project, make sure that you have enough time, enough jars, enough ingredients, enough lids, and enough paraffin. Generally speaking, 2 pounds of fruit require about 2 pounds or 4 cups of sugar and about 2 hours of processing. This, of course is only a rule of thumb. Read each recipe carefully before starting; some preserves take 2 or 3 days to complete. The yield is also highly variable; again, check the recipe and prepare one or two extra jars—stopping to sterilize extras when the end is in sight is infuriating.

When you've ascertained that you have enough of everything, clear and clean the countertop around your stove. Set up all the necessary equipment, especially those small utensils. If your slotted spoon is in your toddler's sandbox, you'll want to know it before you get started. At this point, I put down a double sheet of newspaper on either side of the stove top. This is not very elegant, but it makes cleanup very simple and gives you a place to cool your hot jars. Have handy a few clean cloths to wipe the rims of the jars—the kitchen sponge won't do. Use the same damp cloths to wipe off the jars while they are still hot—much easier than waiting for the spills to harden as they cool.

Keep a bowl or basin of warm soapy water in the sink to put used utensils into. They will be ready effortlessly for another go around.

Now, with the preliminaries out of the way, what will you be making?

Jellies are made by extracting the juices from fruits by first cooking the fruit, then straining the juice through a jelly bag. The bag must not be squeezed: squeezing may increase the yield, but it can also cause the jelly to be cloudy. The juice obtained is then cooked down with sugar to the jelling point. Jellies should be clear and sparkling and hold their shape yet be easy to spread.

Jams consist of whole, chopped, or crushed fruit cooked in one step with sweetener until thick. They need not jell firmly, but should mound together and not "weep."

Marmalades are similar to jams in that they contain identifiable bits of fruit, but the fruit is suspended in a jelly. Marmalades are often more time-consuming to make than jams, particularly the citrus varieties, which require overnight soaking and long, slow cooking of the fruit to tenderize the rinds.

Preserves and conserves are pieces of fruit, whole or cut up, that retain something of their original shape, and are cooked until translucent in heavy syrup. In addition, conserves can contain other ingredients such as nuts and raisins, which tend to retain their identity in cooking.

Butters are thick purees, usually spiced and often dark in color. This is an excellent use for damaged and overripe fruits.

Curds are creamy blends of fruit, butter, and eggs. Because of the eggs, curds must be cooked over boiling water in a double boiler, and a boiling water bath is recommended for processing.

Sweeteners

Sugar is the preserving agent in jams and jellies, granulated white sugar being, of course, the most commonly used sweetener. Generally speaking, sugar is used in the amount of 1½–2 cups for every pound or 2 cups of prepared fruit being preserved. Brown sugar, light or dark, firmly packed, may be substituted for part of the sugar; however, brown sugar tends to mask rather than enhance the flavor of the fruit, and your preserves will be uniformly dark brown.

Honey lends an exquisite flavor of its own to mild-flavored preserves. It can be substituted for up to half of the sugar at the rate of 1 cup of honey for 1¼ cups of sugar. Likewise, maple syrup may be used as part of the sweetener, at the rate of ¾ cup for each cup of sugar required. I will confess to never using maple syrup, the cost being prohibitive; perhaps it is more feasible if you make your own syrup. At any rate, using either maple syrup or honey will lengthen your cooking time, due to the extra liquid content.

Jam sugar (*sucre à confiture*) is relatively new on the market, and in fact may be difficult to find in your local store. It radically simplifies the jam-making process: each pound of this sugar contains 3 or 4 grams of pectin and about 3 grams of citric acid. There is no need to increase the amount of sugar as with commercial pectins. In general, about 2 cups of jam sugar are needed per pound of fruit. Cooking is confined to the raw fruit, with 4 or 5 minutes of boiling after addition of the sugar. The fruit tends to keep its color and savor as well as more of its nutritive value. This is a *very* tempting prospect for devoted "preservers."

Pectin

Pectin is mysterious stuff, occurring naturally to some degree in all fruits, primarily in and near the skins, but also in the pips. When the fruit is cooked with sugar, the pectin is released and acts with the acids of the fruit and the sugar to form jelly, or to "set" the preserve. If you cannot find a recipe to make a preserve of a given fruit, you can test for pectin, add sugar and lemon or apple juice if necessary, according to the results of your test, and so create your own recipe. The test: simmer a small amount of the fruit until tender. Cool and put a tablespoon of the juice obtained in a glass with 1 tablespoon of grain alcohol. Shake gently and observe.

If the fruit is rich in pectin, a single, transparent globule of jelly will form. You will need a cup of sugar for each cup or ½ pound of fruit.

If pectin is present in moderate amounts, several separate globs will form. You will need about ¾ cup of sugar for each cup or ½ pound of fruit.

If the pectin content is very low, numerous small particles of jelly will form. You will need about ½ cup of sugar for each cup or ½ pound of fruit. At this point I generally get out the commercial pectin and start experimenting.

Discard all test samples; do not put them back in the juice. If you use commercial pectins, always choose a very large pot to avoid boil-overs. The pot should be at least large enough to hold four times the amount of fruit and sugar in your recipe.

PECTIN CHART

This chart lists the relative amounts of pectin occurring in some of the more commonly preserved fruits.

HIGH	MEDIUM	LOW
Apples	Apricots	Blueberries
Cranberries	Blackberries	Cherries
Currants	Greengages	Elderberries
Damsons	Loganberries	Figs
Gooseberries	Peaches	Grapes
Lemons	Plums (sweet)	Pears
Plums (tart)	Raspberries	Pineapples
Quinces		Rhubarb
		Strawberries
		Vegetables

In general there is more pectin to be found in tart and in slightly underripe fruits. Low pectin may be remedied by the addition of apple juice in the amount of ¼ cup for each 2 pounds of fruit, or lemon juice at the rate of 1 tablespoon for 2 pounds of fruit. Commercial pectins may be used, following the manufacturers' instructions precisely. Keep in mind, however, that you will need more sugar, sometimes up to 50% more. The less sugar you use, the truer the flavor of your preserve will be; conversely, the flavor will be adversely affected by the use of additional sugar.

On the other hand, the use of commercial pectins greatly decreases the cooking time and increases the yield. The choice is yours.

Spices

Experiment with your favorite spice, by all means, but do it with a light touch. It is too easy to overwhelm the true fruit flavor of your preserves. To retain the color and clarity of your preserves, use whole spices or herbs tied up in a muslin bag, or simply in a piece of sheeting. This saves time at the end of cooking, too, when you would have to skim loose spices out.

Fruits

Ideally, the fruit or other produce being preserved should be picked early in the day, as soon as the dew dries. Then you can run it into the kitchen, clean it off with a towel and proceed to preserve it. If this does not sound like the same planet you currently inhabit, do not despair. Choose the freshest fruits available, and preferably at the height of their season. Wash them carefully and pick over them. Slightly underripe fruits will have more pectin than the dead ripe ones, and often a better flavor when cooked, too. Blemished fruits may be used, but the blemishes should be cut away and discarded.

Fillers

Although "fillers" (fruits used in addition to the primary ingredients to provide body or background flavor) are scorned by purists, it is handy to know how, when, and why to use them. For instance, the British have many recipes for preserving marrow, which is a larger version of zucchini. One begins to understand the need to use them up when those three rows you plant produce enough to feed the entire neighborhood. Marrow or zucchini can be flavored by the addition of fruits, spices, and alcohols. Apples as fillers will add flavor and pectin as well as stretching the yield of your primary fruit.

Be judicious in such additions in order not to dilute the flavor of the primary fruit beyond recognition.

Sterilizing

Before you begin cooking, assemble your jars and lids. Fill the jars three-quarters full of water and place the lids loosely on top. Set the jars in a pan partly filled with water in such a way that the jars don't touch each other; bring to a boil and simmer for 15–20 minutes, then keep the jars warm until ready to be filled. Some cooks do not feel that more than a quick scalding of the jars is necessary, since most preserves require more than 10 minutes of processing (enough to prevent contamination) anyway. I personally prefer to sterilize all jars.

Boiling Water Bath

Not many jams require a boiling water bath, as they almost all require more than 10 minutes of processing by the open kettle method. However, if your peace of mind requires this step, if the jam was processed for less than 10 minutes, or if it has tomatoes in it, here's how: place the filled closed jars in a rack so that they do not touch each other, then place the rack in the bottom of a deep kettle half-filled with boiling water. Add hot or boiling water until the jars are covered by more than an inch of water. Proceed to boil for the required time. When that time has elapsed, lift out the rack and cool the jars on a rack in a place free of drafts.

Now You're Cooking: Generic Hints

Your surfaces are clean and clear; your equipment is lined up; your jars and lids are being sterilized. You're on your way. You may wish to warm your sugar at low heat in the oven. It will dissolve faster and not reduce the heat of your fruit so much when added to it.

Wash all fruit carefully just before preserving. Drain as dry as possible in a colander or on towels. Discard all damaged and bruised portions of the fruit. Proceed with stemming, slicing, coring, and peeling. Crush berries and other small fruits; cut very large ones into uniformly sized pieces. To remove large stones, you may simply halve the fruit: the stones will free themselves in cooking and can then be skimmed from the surface. It is a good idea when doing this to count the fruit and tally this number with the stones you skim. Plum pits on toast can lead to unpleasant breakfasts; the inner pits of peaches can be downright toxic (they contain cyanide).

Do not try to make more than 6 cups of jam at a time, or 4 cups of jelly. If you are trying a new recipe, go for a small quantity. Most of the recipes that follow are for optimal quantities and may be halved. Check the yields before starting.

Start cooking your fruit over low heat to prevent sticking. A further aid is a bit of butter (¼ teaspoon) in the bottom of the pot. Stir occasionally unless you are specifically told not to. Cover the pot only when so instructed, for instance, in the "juicing up" phase, but not in the "cooling down."

The cooking times given in the recipes may not always seem accurate to the minute. There are many variables that will affect the amount of time necessary to make a preserve set, such as the age of the produce; the size of the slices or chunks of fruit; the amount of liquid called for, which is often stated as "enough to be seen through the top layer of fruit, but not enough to float it"; the type of stove being used; the degree of heat (bolder cooking requires less time, but is riskier); and the prewarming of the sugar. I have at different times had to add as much as 45 minutes to the cooking time of a recipe or found the jam ready to set with the jars not yet completely sterilized. It is wise therefore to have everything ready in advance, and also to leave ample time before your next appointment.

Occasionally, a recipe will require reduction of the quantity in a saucepan by a third or a half. This is easier to measure than it sounds: simply mark the handle of a wooden spoon with a small knife cut at the outset; then check regularly until the required reduction is achieved.

Jelly: the Generic Recipe

The rule of thumb when assembling equipment for jelly-making is that 2 pounds of prepared fruit will yield about 4 cups of juice, which, with the sugar added, will give you 3 cups of jelly, or two 12-ounce jars.

In general, there is no need to pare the fruit, except pineapples. Indeed, it is best to cook the skins too, as most of the pectin is found there. Cut large fruits into pieces, smaller ones in half. Most need not be cored. Crush berries and soft fruits.

When adding water, add the minimum necessary to prevent sticking. For larger fruits, add enough water to be seen through the top layer: the fruit should not be afloat.

Now, bring your saucepan to a boil, cover, and cook until the juices run freely.

Jelly necessarily takes longer than jam because you cannot rush the straining process. Make sure your jelly bag is clean, but do not wash it with detergents. Scald it before each use. Place your cooked fruit in the bag and leave it to strain overnight. In order to obtain a sparkling clear jelly, do not squeeze the bag. Let the process happen naturally. You may, in fact, wish to do a preliminary straining through a colander, and the final straining through a jelly bag.

In the morning, measure the juice and put it in a large heavy-bottomed pot. Bring to a boil and cook for 5 minutes before adding the prewarmed sugar, stirring until it dissolves. Bring to a full boil and cook from 10 to 30 minutes, depending on your recipe. Begin testing for set after 10 minutes.

To test jelly for set, scoop out a spoonful and tilt the spoon sideways over the pot. If the syrup runs off in a single stream, it is not ready. When the spoon coats and the product drops off in a sheet, or if two blobs form at the rim at once, it is ready. Skim off the foam and pour the jelly into hot jars that are as dry as possible.

Jam: the Generic Recipe

Once you have followed the general hints listed above, measure the prepared fruit. At this point, there is a choice: you may put the fruit in the pan with a small amount of water and bring it to a boil, or you may pour the required amount of sugar over the fruit in a bowl and allow the mixture to stand until the fruit juices up naturally.

Proceed to cook the jam, gently or furiously as required by the recipe. A rapid boil preserves both color and flavor. Stir only as needed to prevent sticking.

After 10 minutes, unless the recipe specifies a longer cooking time, begin testing for set. This involves putting a small amount of preserve on a cold saucer. When the jam cools, push it with your finger. The surface will wrinkle when the jam is ready to set. If the jam refuses to set, don't give up: try adding a tablespoon or so of lemon juice and cooking a bit longer.

If there is too much syrup and you wish to preserve the integrity of your fruit, both in flavor and color, skim out the fruit when it is cooked and boil down the syrup. Return the fruit to the pan briefly to heat it through. Otherwise, cool the jam before transferring it to the jars, stirring occasionally to prevent floating fruit.

Skim off any foam, spices, or pits on the surface. A small bit of butter at this point will help to dissipate that last stubborn trace of foam. Ladle the jam into sterilized jars (I use a metal ½-cup measure to do this). Fill the jars to the bottom of the neck, leaving about ¼-inch headspace. This latter is simply the space at the top of the jar. You do not want to have the level of the jam below the neck, particularly if you are using paraffin: you will never get the paraffin out. Nor should the preserves be too near the rim.

The homestretch consists of wiping the rims of the jars clean using a clean damp cloth. If you are using "collected jars" as opposed to the standard purchased ones, pour ⅛ inch of melted paraffin (see page 13) on the surface of the jam at this time. Put the lids on and tighten down when the paraffin cools. Do not use the inversion method to complete the seal. If you are using standardized jars, place the new disk on top followed by the reusable band. Clean the outside of your jars of spills and dribbles at this point: do not wait for them to cool and harden on the jars. To create a vacuum seal by the inversion method, tighten the lids down and invert the jars for a few minutes, then place the jars right-side up on towels, paper, or racks to cool. When the jars are cold, check the seals by pressing on the center of the lid: there should be a slight concavity and no popping. Finally, label them with their contents and date of preserving. Most jams and jellies have a shelf life of 1 year, unless otherwise specified. Note on the label any expiration date short of 1 year.

Store in a cool, dry place, preferably in the dark, then proceed to use up your preserves as methodically as you put them up: move the older preserves to the front and the newer ones to the back.

The Trouble-Shooter's Guide

"The best laid schemes o' mice and men gang aft a-gley," as Robert Burns said "To a Mouse," but we are talking about preserves here.

If the jam seizes up and you find yourself with a jar full of rubber cement, you have more than one recourse: you can return it to the pan, add a small amount of water to dilute it, cook it briefly, then follow the potting procedures described above; or you can wait until you need it as a sauce, heat it gently with a little brandy or other alcohol suitable to the flavor of the fruit. Or give it to the children to use as paste—don't you worry about the edibility of their paste?

In the same vein, if the jelly simply won't jell, first try adding extra pectin in the form of apple juice or lemon juice as described above. If all else fails, use it as a syrup, perhaps adding a little zing with some extra lemon juice or an alcohol.

A bitter ingredient can be neutralized at least partially by the addition of a small amount of brandy toward the end of the cooking period.

A cloudy jelly is probably the result of the jelly bag having been squeezed. If you can't bear cloudy jelly, try reheating and re-straining the juice through a double layer of muslin.

Cloudy jam or marmalade may result from not using enough sugar. Recalculate and add more, if necessary. In any case, a jam with too little sugar will not keep well.

Crystallized jams are lacking in citric acid. Recook with added lemon juice or vinegar.

Fermented preserves result from a too-brief cooking; the situation can be corrected by recooking.

Mold has many causes. Perhaps the jars were not tightly sealed, or the storage area is too warm or too damp. If you catch this situation before the damage is too far advanced, i.e., you're not dealing with a thick furry coating of the stuff, you may remove the mold, reheat, and reseal with hot paraffin. This is a matter of aesthetics.

Serious spoilage, discoloration, and off odors indicate a preserve beyond help. Discard all such, but keep the jars. Do not lightly discard the fruits of your labor except in the last-mentioned circumstances.

Now, go to it. Preserving can be fun, and the spirits of your forebears will be pleased that this lore persists. There will come a summery day when a child will bring you a hatful of juicy but seedy dewberries, and you will know just what to do with them. And she will love you all the better for your wisdom.

FEIJOA JELLY (SEE PAGE 93)

The
Recipes

Out of the Orchard

Paradise Jelly

Yield: about 8 cups

This is a jelly with an unparalleled desire to please: the purply red color is heavenly, like its name, and it sets quickly, with no trouble.

✂ INGREDIENTS ✂

5 medium-size tart apples (Green MacIntosh or Granny Smith)

3 quinces

12 ounces cranberries

sugar

Wash all the fruit. Cut the apples in quarters; coarsely chop the quinces; pick over the cranberries and discard any damaged ones. Put all the fruit in a pan and add water to cover.

Bring to a boil and simmer, covered, until soft, about 45 minutes. Strain overnight through a jelly bag.

In the morning, measure the juice obtained. Cooking only 4 cups of juice at a time, bring to a boil and cook for 5 minutes. Skim; add 1 cup of sugar for each cup of juice in the pan, stirring until dissolved. Return to a boil and cook briskly until ready to set. Begin testing for set after 5 minutes.

Remove from heat; ladle into hot sterilized jars, leaving ¼-inch headspace. Wipe the rims clean, put the lids in place, and tighten down. Invert the jars for a few minutes, then turn them upright again and let cool completely. Check the seals, label, and store in a cool, dry place.

Apple Butter

Yield: about 4 cups

This is an excellent use for the pulp left after making apple jelly; you may also use fresh apples, or a combination of the two. The keeping quality of the butter will be improved if you add ½ cup of sugar, white or brown, at the beginning of the cooking-down process.

Blackberry Nectarine Jam

Yield: about 4 cups

Carefully stirring the blackberries while cooking helps to keep the berries nearly intact, while imparting a lovely pink tinge to the jam.

✄ INGREDIENTS ✄

2 pounds cooking apples (or 1 quart cooked apple pulp)
½ teaspoon cinnamon
¼ teaspoon ground cloves
¼ teaspoon ground allspice
sweet cider

If you are using fresh apples, wash, peel, and quarter them and place in a pan with the spices and enough sweet cider to cover. Bring slowly to a boil. Mash the apples with a wooden spoon and cook until you have a dark, smooth, buttery jam.

If you are using the cooked pulp left over from jelly-making, stir in 2 cups of sweet cider per quart of pulp. Force through a sieve or colander, then add the spices, bring slowly to a boil, and cook as above.

In either case, when you have achieved a dark, thick butter, pot it in sterile jars, leaving ¼-inch headspace. Wipe the rims clean, put the lids in place, and tighten down. If you have not included sugar in the recipe, subject the jars to a 10-minute boiling water bath. Remove from the kettle and let cool completely. Check the seals, label, and store in a cool, dry place.

✄ INGREDIENTS ✄

½ pound blackberries
3 pounds nectarines, not too ripe
2 apples
1 lemon
1½ cups water
6 cups sugar

Wash the blackberries and set aside to drain dry. Wash and peel the nectarines; cut into pieces, discarding the pits. Peel, quarter, and core the apples. Reserve the apple peel, tying it up in a muslin bag, and chop the flesh. Put the nectarines and apples in a saucepan with the water and the apple peel. Bring to a boil, cover, and cook until the fruit is very tender, about 20 minutes. Remove the muslin bag and mash the fruit with

a wooden spoon. Add the lemon juice and sugar, a cup at a time, stirring until dissolved. Return to a boil; cook briskly until nearly set (about 15 minutes) before adding the blackberries. Continue to cook until set, stirring carefully from time to time.

When ready to set, ladle the jam into hot sterilized jars, leaving ¼-inch headspace. Wipe the rims clean, put the lids in place, and tighten down. Invert the jars for a few minutes, then return to the upright and let cool completely. Check the seals, label, and store in a cool, dry place.

Rosemary- Quince Jelly

Yield: about 4 cups

✄ INGREDIENTS ✄

4 pounds quinces (about 8)

juice of 2 lemons

sugar (about 4 cups)

2 tablespoons chopped rosemary

4 3-inch sprigs rosemary

Wash the quinces and coarsely chop, removing the stem and blossom ends. Place in a pan with the lemon juice. Cover with water, bring to a boil, and simmer, covered, until the quinces are very tender, about 45 minutes. Strain through a jelly bag overnight.

In the morning, measure the juice, return it to the pan, and add 1 cup of sugar per cup of juice, stirring until the sugar dissolves. Boil briskly for about 5 minutes, then begin testing for set.

When ready to set, stir in the chopped rosemary; place 1 sprig of rosemary in each sterilized jar before ladling in the jelly, leaving ¼-inch headspace. Wipe the rims clean, put the lids in place, and tighten down. Invert the jars for a few moments, then return to the upright and let cool completely. Check the seals, label, and store in a cool, dry place.

Apple and Rhubarb Jam

Yield: about 4 cups

Here is a wonderful jam: quick and easy to make, good yield, dainty pink in color, redolent of apples and rhubarb. The color comes from using red rhubarb, but if you have a choice, try the green; the flavor is much better. Good as it is plain, this jam fairly begs to be spiced with your favorite flavors: nutmeg and clove come to mind—experiment, but with a light touch.

✄ INGREDIENTS ✄

1 pound apples

1 pound rhubarb

⅓ cup water

3 cups sugar

Peel, core, and chop the apples. Wash, dry, trim, and chop the rhubarb. Put the fruit in a large saucepan with the water; heat gently, then simmer until tender, about 20 minutes. Check often to see that no sticking occurs; at this stage the moisture is minimal indeed. When tender, add the sugar, stirring until dissolved. Boil rapidly at first, then more carefully until set (about 20 minutes), stirring frequently. This is a "spitter," so you may want to partially cover the pot as the jam cooks down.

Ladle into hot sterilized jars, leaving ¼-inch headspace. Wipe the rims clean, put the lids in place, and tighten down. Invert the jars for a few minutes, then return to the upright and let cool completely. Check the seals, label, and store in a cool, dry place.

APPLE AND RHUBARB JAM MAKES AN EXCELLENT ACCOMPANIMENT FOR PORK CHOPS.

Carrot, Apple, and Peach Marmalade

Yield: about 4 cups

Here is a good, old-fashioned British-type marmalade. The original cooking instructions are to put all ingredients in a pot and boil until clear. Simple, but with a minimum of refinement, the results are infinitely superior.

✂ INGREDIENTS ✂

1 pound carrots (3 large)

½ pound peaches

1 pound apples

juice of 1 lemon

3 cups sugar

6 cloves

2 tablespoons dark rum (optional)

Peel and dice the carrots; place in a saucepan with a minimum of water and cook until tender (about 15 minutes). Meanwhile, wash and dice the unpeeled peaches (discard the pits), and peel, core, and dice the apples. When the carrots are tender, add the prepared fruit to the pan with the lemon juice and the sugar. Bring slowly back to a boil, stirring until all the sugar dissolves. Add the cloves and boil rapidly until the jam is clear and set. Reduce the heat toward the end of the cooking and stir frequently to avoid sticking. Remove from the heat and gradually add the rum, if desired.

Ladle into hot sterilized jars, leaving ¼-inch headspace. Wipe the rims clean, put the lids in place, and tighten down. Invert the jars for a few minutes, then return to the upright, shaking firmly to eliminate air bubbles. Let cool completely. Check the seals, label, and store in a cool, dry place.

CARROT, APPLE, AND PEACH
MARMALADE

Apricot and Cherry Jam

Yield: about 5 cups

✄ INGREDIENTS ✄

2 pounds apricots

1 pound cherries

½ cup water

6 cups sugar

juice of 2 lemons

Wash the fruit; remove the apricot stones and cherry pits. Place the fruit in a saucepan with ½ cup water. Cover and simmer until tender. Then add the sugar and lemon juice, stirring until the sugar is dissolved. Boil rapidly to set, about 20 minutes.

Ladle into hot sterilized jars, leaving ¼-inch headspace. Wipe the rims clean, put the lids in place, and tighten down. Invert the jars for a few minutes, then return to the upright and let cool completely. Check the seals, label, and store in a cool, dry place.

Cherry-Cherry Jam

Yield: about 5 cups

The flavor is enhanced both by cooking the pits and by adding the kirsch.

✄ INGREDIENTS ✄

2 pounds cherries

3 cups sugar

1 lemon

2 tablespoons kirsch

Rinse, stem, and pit the cherries; tie the cherry pits up in a muslin bag. Simmer the cherries and pits in 2 tablespoons of water until soft (10–15 minutes). Remove the bag of pits, stir in the sugar, and boil rapidly until set, about 15 minutes longer. At the last minute, add the kirsch, 1 tablespoon at a time, then remove at once from the heat.

Ladle the jam into hot sterilized jars, leaving ¼-inch headspace. Wipe the rims clean, put the lids in place, and tighten down. Invert the jars for a few minutes, then return to the upright and let cool completely. Check the seals, label, and store in a cool, dry place.

Apricot Conserve

Yield: about 5 cups

This recipe yields quick, simple, and utterly delicious results.

✂ INGREDIENTS ✂

2 pounds apricots

4 cups sugar

juice of 2 lemons

Wash, quarter, and stone the apricots. Place them in a heavy-bottomed saucepan with the sugar and the lemon juice. Heat gently, stirring constantly until the sugar dissolves, then boil carefully until set. This conserve has a tendency to stick if you don't pay attention, but the cooking time start to finish is brief and the result so good that it's worth hovering over the pot.

When set, ladle into hot sterilized jars, leaving ¼-inch head-space. Wipe the rims clean, put the lids in place, and tighten down. Invert the jars for a few minutes, then return to the upright and let cool completely. Check the seals, label, and store in a cool, dry place.

Madeira Plum Jam

Yield: about 4½ cups

✂ INGREDIENTS ✂

2 pounds ripe red plums

1 cup water

3 cups sugar

2 sticks cinnamon

½ cup Madeira

Wash, halve, and stone the plums. Put the water and 1½ cups sugar in a pan. Bring to a boil, stirring until the sugar dissolves. Boil 5 minutes without stirring. Add the prepared plums, return to the boil, and cook for 20 minutes, or until the fruit is soft and pulpy. Stir occasionally to prevent sticking. When the fruit is soft, add the remaining sugar and the cinnamon. Cook without stirring until nearly set, about 20 minutes longer. If necessary, drag a wooden spoon gently across the bottom from time to time to prevent sticking. Add the Madeira and simmer until set.

Ladle into hot sterilized jars, leaving ¼-inch headspace. Wipe the rims clean, put the lids in place, and tighten down. Process 10 minutes in a boiling water bath. Remove from the bath and invert for a few minutes, then return to the upright and let cool completely. Check the seals, label, and store in a cool, dry place.

Peach Jam

Yield: about 6 cups

PEACHES

❌ INGREDIENTS ❌

6 pounds peaches, ripe but firm and unblemished

3 lemons

1 cup water

6 cups sugar

Wash the peaches, remove the pits, and dice the unpeeled fruit. Extract the juice from the lemons; make a few thin slices of the outer peel of 1 lemon, with no pith. Place the peaches, lemon juice, and lemon peel in a saucepan with the water and the sugar. Bring slowly to a boil, stirring constantly until all the sugar dissolves. Continue to cook and stir very gently until set, about 20 minutes; this jam tends to stick and scorch as it cooks down so pay attention!

When thick enough to set, remove the pieces of lemon rind and ladle the jam into sterilized jars, leaving ¼-inch headspace. Wipe the rims clean, put the lids in place, and tighten down. Invert the jars briefly, then return to the upright, shaking firmly to eliminate air bubbles. Let cool completely. Check the seals, label, and store in a cool, dry place.

Quince Jam

Yield: about 5 cups

The quince is a good old-fashioned fruit with a heavenly perfume and amazing keeping qualities when refrigerated. However, it browns very rapidly when peeled, and though it looks like a pear, it lacks the latter's pliant nature: it is woody and positively resists chopping. Once subdued by the persistent cook, it submits meekly and turns into a delicious jam, loaded with pectin.

✂ INGREDIENTS ✂

4 quinces

1½ lemons

4 cups sugar

QUINCES

Peel and core the quinces. Boil the cores and peels for 3 minutes in water to cover. Meanwhile, soak the quince flesh in a bowl of cold water with the juice of ½ lemon to prevent discoloration. Drain and cool the cooked liquid; discard the peels and cores. Finely chop the quinces, put in the pan with the previously cooked liquid, and simmer just until tender (15–20 minutes). Boil off most of the liquid before adding the juice of 1 lemon. Stir in the sugar until dissolved and boil rapidly until set.

Ladle into hot sterilized jars, leaving ¼-inch headspace. Wipe the rims clean, put the lids in place, and tighten down. Invert the jars for a few minutes, then return to the upright and let cool completely. Check the seals, label, and store in a cool, dry place.

Red-Hot Quince Jam

Follow the recipe for quince jam, stirring in 2 tablespoons of red hot candies just before the end of the cooking. Use more red hots for a stronger flavor and deeper color. Stir until all the candies are dissolved (this takes a few minutes) or remove from the heat while there are still gooey bits of candy in suspension.

Follow the usual potting procedure.

Heavenly Jam

Yield: about 5 cups

Why "heavenly"? The maraschino pink color of this old New England recipe is out of this world, the flavor divine: altogether a recipe worth resurrecting. Note that the quantities are expressed entirely in threes.

✄ INGREDIENTS ✄

3 pounds peaches

3 pounds sugar (6 cups)

3 oranges

3-ounce jar maraschino cherries (about ~~12~~ *10—* cherries, with the liquid to cover)

Peel, pit, and mash the peaches with a potato masher or ricer. Fine-chopping with a knife is also acceptable, but do not puree. In a bowl, cover the peaches with the sugar, put a lid on the bowl, and let stand several hours, or overnight.

[handwritten: dicing is nice + leaves chunks]

When the juice has been released from the fruits, put the peaches and sugar in a saucepan: add to this the grated rind

of 1 well-washed orange; the pulp and juice of all 3 oranges; the cherries, cut *[handwritten: diced]* into pieces but not too finely; and the maraschino juice. Bring slowly to a boil and cook until thickened, about 30 minutes. Be sure to stir occasionally as the mixture thickens to prevent sticking.

[handwritten: pull all pulp from insides after juicing]

Ladle into hot sterilized jars, leaving ¼-inch headspace. Wipe the rims clean, put the lids in place, and tighten down. Invert the jars for a few minutes to complete the seal, then return to the upright and let cool completely. Check the seals, label, and store in a cool, dry place.

Apple Jelly

Yield: about 5 cups

This is the ultimate "basic" jelly, the perfect vehicle for your favorite herbs or blossoms.

✄ INGREDIENTS ✄

4 pounds tart apples (Green MacIntosh or Granny Smith)

sugar

Wash and stem the apples; roughly chop the skins, cores, seeds, and all. Put in a large pot with water just to cover.

Bring to a boil and simmer, covered, until the apples are *very* soft, 30–45 minutes.

Strain through a jelly bag for several hours, or overnight. For a clear jelly, avoid squeezing the bag. If discarding all that juicy pulp bothers you, save the pulp and use it for apple butter or apple-apricot butter.

Measure the juice obtained. Do not process more than 4 cups at a time. Place the juice in a large saucepan; boil for 20 minutes, then add 1 cup of sugar for each cup of juice measured into the pot. Stir until the sugar is dissolved, then boil rapidly for 5 minutes.

Begin testing for set; when the jelly sheets from the spoon, pour it into hot sterilized jars, leaving ¼-inch head-space. Wipe the rims clean, put the lids in place, and tighten down. Invert the jars for a few minutes to complete the seal, then return to the upright and let cool completely. Check the seals, label, and store in a cool, dry place.

Rose Geranium Jelly

Yield: about 5 cups

Follow the recipe for apple jelly, adding 2–3 rose geranium leaves per pint of juice when you add the sugar. Discard these cooked leaves when you fill the jars, but add 1 fresh leaf to each jar before sealing. Follow the usual potting procedure. Any favorite herb may be substituted for the rose geranium leaves.

Apple Jam

Yield: about 5 cups

MacIntoshes tend to mush up nicely when cooked; Granny Smiths keep their shape a little better. Combine the two for a smooth basic jam with surprising little bits of tartness.

✄ INGREDIENTS ✄

2½ pounds apples (5 medium size), mixed MacIntoshes and Granny Smith, or other tart variety

juice of 1 lemon

2¾ cups sugar

2 tablespoons lemon juice

cinnamon and clove to taste

Quarter, peel, and core the apples. Keep the quartered apples in a bowl of water with the juice of 1 lemon to prevent discoloration. Place the cores and peels in a saucepan with water to cover, and cook until mush, 15–20 minutes. Strain off and reserve the pulp and juice. This step may be eliminated and the peels and cores discarded, but remember that much of the pectin is near the skin of the apple (and some in the seeds), and the more pectin involved, the less cooking down required to obtain a set.

When ready to continue cooking, drain and finely chop the apples. Place the apples in a saucepan with the juice and pulp obtained by cooking the peels and cores. Add water until it can be seen through the top layer of apples. Cover and cook until very soft, about 20 minutes. Mash partially if necessary. When mashed to the desired consistency, add the sugar, 2 tablespoons of lemon juice, and the spices, stirring until all the sugar is dissolved. Continue to cook until thick.

Ladle into hot sterilized jars, leaving ¼-inch headspace. Wipe the rims clean, put the lids in place, and tighten down. Invert the jars for a few minutes to complete the seal, then return to the upright and let cool completely. Check the seals, label, and store in a cool, dry place.

Spearmint and Apple Jam

Yield: about 3 cups

Peppermint may be substituted if you prefer; the color of the jam will be much darker and hardly in need of the food coloring.

✄ INGREDIENTS ✄

2 pounds apples
4 ounces fresh spearmint leaves
2½ cups sugar
green food coloring (optional)

Peel, core, and finely chop the apples. Place in a saucepan with enough water to be just visible through the top layer of fruit. Cover, and cook until the apples are very soft, about 20 minutes. Add the spearmint leaves, rinsed and chopped up very finely. Cook, uncovered, for 15 minutes; when well-scented, force through a sieve or process in a blender or food processor. Return to the pot, add 2½ cups sugar, and simmer until set. Stir frequently to prevent sticking. When the jam is thick and smooth, add 3–4 drops of green food coloring to brighten the color.

Ladle into hot sterilized jars, leaving ¼-inch headspace. Wipe the rims clean, put the lids in place, and tighten down. Invert the jars for a few minutes, then return to the upright and let cool completely. Check the seals, label, and store in a cool, dry place.

SPEARMINT AND APPLE JAM

Chocolate Apple Butter

Yield: about 5 cups

This makes a great filling for a layer cake, or a wonderful snack spread on bread.

✂ INGREDIENTS ✂

3 pounds apples

1½ lemons

½ cup water

¾ cup cocoa powder

4½ cups sugar

4-inch vanilla bean pod

2 tablespoons Cointreau or Grand Marnier (optional)

Peel, core, and chop the apples. If you wish to use the apple peel for added pectin, peel the apples in long strips. Grate the rind of the lemons and squeeze the juice. Put the apples, the peel (if using), the lemon rind, and the lemon juice into a saucepan with the water and cook together gently until the apples are very tender, about 20 minutes. Remove the peel

at this point, if you have used it. Sieve or process the pulp until smooth, then return it to the pot.

Toss the cocoa powder and sugar together; stir the sugar-cocoa powder mixture into the apple puree until it is completely dissolved; add the vanilla bean and continue to cook gently, stirring constantly until thick and smooth. When the jam responds favorably to the saucer test, remove from the heat. At this point, remove the vanilla bean and quickly stir in the orange liqueur.

Ladle into hot sterilized jars, leaving ¼-inch headspace. Eliminate air bubbles with a nonmetallic spatula. Wipe the rims clean, put the lids in place, and tighten down. Shake the jars firmly to further settle the contents. Let cool completely. Check the seals, label, and store in a cool, dry place.

Apple and Apricot Butter

Yield: about 2 cups

This is a classic use-it-upper, albeit a scrumptious one. Use the spices you like, but in quantities that don't overwhelm the apricots. Alter the proportions to suit what you have on hand.

✂ I N G R E D I E N T S ✂

1 pound pulp from apple jelly (or 1 pound fresh apples)

1 pound apricots

per cup puree:

½ cup sugar

juice of ½ lemon

small grating of lemon peel

¼ teaspoon ground clove

¼ teaspoon ground allspice

½ teaspoon cinnamon

1 tablespoon brandy (optional)

If you are using fresh apples, wash, stem, quarter, and roughly chop. Put in a saucepan with enough water just to be visible through the top layer of fruit. Wash, peel, pit, and quarter the apricots, and add them to the apples. Bring to a boil and cook until quite pulpy, about 20 minutes.

If you are using the pulp from apple jelly-making, start by washing, peeling, pitting, and quartering the apricots. Place in a saucepan with a small amount of water and cook until very soft. Stir in the apple pulp with a small quantity of water if necessary.

In either case, at this point force the cooked fruit through a sieve, measure the puree and add, per cup, ½ cup sugar, the juice of ½ lemon, and a small grating of lemon peel. Return to the saucepan, and add the spices to taste. Stir together until the sugar dissolves, then let simmer very slowly until glossy and thick. When ready to set, add 1 tablespoon brandy, if desired.

Ladle into hot sterilized jars, leaving ¼-inch headspace. Wipe the rims clean, put the lids in place, and tighten down. Invert the jars for a few minutes, then return to the upright. Shake firmly to eliminate air bubbles. Let cool completely. Check the seals, label, and store in a cool, dry place.

Sherry Cherry Berry Jam

Yield: about 4 cups

✂ I N G R E D I E N T S ✂

1 pound cherries

1 pound strawberries

2⅔ cups sugar

juice of 1½ lemons

3 tablespoons sherry

juice of 2 lemons

Wash all the fruit. Stem and pit the cherries, tying the pits into a muslin bag. Remove the caps from the strawberries and halve the fruit. Place both fruits in a saucepan with the pits. Bring very slowly to a boil and cook gently until the fruit is soft. Remove the bag of pits; stir the sugar into the fruit until dissolved. Add the lemon juice and boil rapidly until set, about 20 minutes, stirring at the end of cooking to prevent sticking.

Add the sherry toward the end of the cooking period, cooking a few minutes longer.

Ladle the jam into hot sterilized jars, leaving ¼-inch headspace. Wipe the rims clean, put the lids in place, and tighten down. Invert the jars for a few minutes, then return to the upright and let cool completely. Check the seals, label, and store in a cool, dry place.

Date 'n' Apple Preserve

Yield: about 4 cups

In spite of the sweetness of the dates,

this preserve has a surprising tartness.

Try it with pound cake and

whipped cream.

✗ INGREDIENTS ✗

1¼ pounds tart cooking apples (Green MacIntosh or Granny Smith)

juice of 1 lemon

6 ounces pitted dates

2 cups sugar

Peel, core, and cut the apples in chunks. Toss with the lemon juice, cover with the sugar, and let stand, covered, overnight.

In the morning, heat the fruit gently, stirring to dissolve the sugar. Chop the dates and add them to the pot. Cook carefully to avoid sticking until very thick, about 30 minutes.

Ladle into hot sterilized jars, using a nonmetallic spatula to eliminate air bubbles. Leave ¼-inch headspace. Wipe the rims clean, put lids in place, and tighten down. Process in a boiling water bath for 10 minutes; remove from the water bath and let cool completely. Check the seals, label, and store in a cool, dry place.

DATE 'N' APPLE PRESERVE MAKES A WONDERFUL COMPLEMENT TO A DISH OF SEARED DUCK BREAST.

Greengage Jam

Yield: about 3½ cups

✂ INGREDIENTS ✂

2 pounds greengages

½ cup water

3 cups sugar

Wash the fruit well. Halve, stem, and remove the stones. Place in a pot with ½ cup of water and simmer for about 15 minutes. Add the sugar, stirring until dissolved, then boil very gently to set. Skim off foam if necessary.

Ladle into hot sterilized jars, leaving ¼-inch headspace. Wipe the rims clean, put the lids in place, and tighten down. Invert the jars for a few minutes, then return to the upright and let cool completely. Check the seals, label, and store in a cool, dry place.

Greengage and Apple Jam

Yield: about 4 cups

A very quick and easy jam; the greengages go further with the addition of the apples, but their flavor is less pronounced. This is a prime candidate for the addition of your favorite spices.

✂ INGREDIENTS ✂

1 pound greengages

½ pound tart apples (MacIntosh or Granny Smith)

¼ cup water

2 cups sugar

Wash the fruit well. Halve the greengages and remove stems and stones. Peel and core the apples; cut into chunks. Place all the fruit in a pot with the water and simmer until soft. (If the greengages are very ripe, cook the apples briefly by themselves to start.) Add the sugar and cloves, stirring until all the sugar is dissolved. Boil steadily until set, about 20 minutes. Skim if necessary, removing the cloves if you wish.

Ladle into hot sterilized jars, leaving ¼-inch headspace. Wipe the rims clean, put the lids in place, and tighten down. Invert the jars for a few minutes, then return to the upright and let cool completely. Check the seals, label, and store in a cool, dry place.

Spiced Black Grape Jelly

Yield: about 4 cups

✂ INGREDIENTS ✂

1 tart apple (MacIntosh or Granny Smith)

3 pounds ripe black grapes

1 cinnamon stick

1 dozen cloves, stems only

½ cup water

sugar

Wash all the fruit well. Cut the apple into quarters. Stem the grapes and cut them in half; this is time-consuming, but it increases the yield of juice and reduces the cooking time, thereby retaining flavor. Crush the grapes in the pot, add the apple, the spices, and the water. Boil about 20 minutes, until the fruit is pulped and the juice runs freely and purple. Strain through a jelly bag overnight.

In the morning, do not squeeze the bag. Measure the juice, then return it to the pot and bring it to a boil. Do not try to cook more than 4 cups of juice at a time. Add ¾ cup of sugar for each cup of juice obtained. Stir until all the sugar is dissolved. Boil rapidly to set, about 40 minutes. Do not overcook.

Ladle into hot sterilized jars, leaving ¼-inch headspace. Wipe the rims clean, put the lids in place, and tighten down. Invert the jars for a few minutes, then return to the upright and let cool completely. Check the seals, label, and store in a cool, dry place.

Green Grape Jam

Yield: about 3 cups

This jam has a pleasant, cool green color and actually tastes tartly of the grapes themselves. If you should happen to slightly scorch it in the final cooking, the jam tastes more of golden raisins than grapes.

✂ I N G R E D I E N T S ✂

1 pound seedless green grapes

juice of 1 lemon

2 cups sugar

Wash the grapes. Place in a pan with a minimal amount of water (⅓ cup) and simmer until tender, about 5 minutes. Puree in a blender or food mill. Return to the pot with the lemon juice and the sugar, stirring until the sugar is dissolved. Boil until set, about 15 minutes, stirring occasionally to prevent sticking. Skim as necessary.

Ladle into hot sterilized jars, leaving ¼-inch headspace. Wipe the rims clean, put the lids in place, and tighten down. Invert the jars for a few minutes, then return to the upright and let cool completely. Check the seals, label, and store in a cool, dry place.

Ginger Pears

Yield: 2 pints (may be tripled)

This is not a proper jam. It is more properly a preserve of ginger slices in a very heavy syrup, and is great as a topping for pound cake, ice cream, or waffles.

✂ I N G R E D I E N T S ✂

3 pounds hard green pears

1 lemon

3⅓ cups sugar

1 ounce crystallized ginger

Peel, core, and slice the pears very thinly. Cut only the outer rind of the lemon in strips, and add to the pears with the juice of the lemon in a pan. Add the sugar and let stand about 1 hour to release the juice from the pears. When the juice has formed, add the ginger, bring to a boil, and simmer gently about 2 hours, until the pears are translucent and the juice sheets from the spoon. Remove the pan from the heat and cool slightly before filling the jars, stirring frequently to prevent floating fruit.

Put into hot sterilized jars, leaving ¼-inch headspace. Wipe the rims clean, put the lids in place, and tighten down. Invert the jars for a few minutes, then return to the upright and let cool completely. Check the seals, label, and store in a cool, dry place.

GINGER PEARS

The Gardener's Revenge

Rhubarb-Prune Jam

Yield: about 6 cups

This is another of life's pleasant surprises: the combination of tartness and sweetness is perfect and the color is a deep clear brown, unlike the brown of fruit butters.

✂ INGREDIENTS ✂

2 pounds pitted prunes

4 pounds rhubarb

5 cups sugar

Day 1: Put the prunes in cold water and set aside to soak overnight. Wash and dry the rhubarb; cut it in small pieces, put it in a bowl, and cover with the sugar. Let stand overnight.

Day 2: Put the rhubarb-sugar mixture in a pot, and bring slowly to a boil, stirring until all the sugar is dissolved. Cook for 40–50 minutes, or until tender (the fresher the fruit, the shorter the cooking time). Drain the prunes, add them to the rhubarb, and continue to cook until thick and deep brown in color. Ladle into hot sterilized jars, leaving ¼–inch headroom. Use a nonmetallic spatula to eliminate air bubbles. Wipe the rims clean, put the lids in place, and tighten down. Check the seals, label, and store in a cool dry place.

PRUNES ARE THE PERFECT COMPANION FOR PORK, MAKING RHUBARB-PRUNE JAM A NATURAL FOR ROAST LOIN.

Strawberry-Rhubarb Jam

Yield: about 6 cups

✂ INGREDIENTS ✂

1 pound rhubarb

7 cups sugar

2 pounds (2 quarts) strawberries

STRAWBERRY-RHUBARB JAM IS THE
FILLING IN THESE SHORTBREAD COOKIES.

Wash and dry the rhubarb stalks, trim 1 inch off each end, and cut the stalks into ½-inch pieces; you should have about 4 cups of cut rhubarb. Place in a large bowl in layers with the sugar; let stand overnight to juice up.

In the morning, wash the berries gently and drain as dry as possible. Remove the stems and caps; cut in half. Place the rhubarb in a pot and bring rapidly to a boil, stirring until all the sugar dissolves; add the prepared berries and cook briskly until set, about 20–25 minutes. Skim off the foam.

Ladle the jam into hot sterilized jars, leaving ¼-inch head-space. Wipe the rims clean, put the lids in place, and tighten down. Invert the jars for a few minutes, then return to the upright and let cool completely. Check the seals, label, and store in a cool, dry place.

Watermelon Rind Preserve

Yield: about 3 cups

✂ INGREDIENTS ✂

2 pounds watermelon rind

2 tablespoons salt

2 cups sugar

2 lemons

¼ cup preserved ginger (or 2 tablespoons powdered ginger)

Pare off the outer rind of the watermelon and remove all trace of the pink flesh. Cut the rind into cubes, place it in a bowl, and cover with the salt and 2 quarts of water. Let stand overnight.

In the morning, drain the watermelon rind, rinse well with cold water, and drain again. Put in a saucepan with just enough boiling water to cover. Cook for 15 minutes, making sure the water doesn't all boil away, causing sticking. Add the sugar and 8 cups more water. Bring to a boil and cook 5 minutes, then add the lemons, very thinly sliced, and the ginger. Cook until the rind is translucent and the syrup thickens, about 30 minutes longer.

Ladle into hot sterilized jars, leaving ¼-inch headspace. Use a nonmetallic spatula to eliminate air bubbles. Wipe the rims clean, put the lids in place, and tighten down. Let cool completely. Check the seals, label, and store in a cool, dry place.

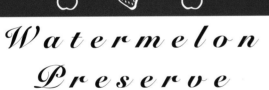

Watermelon Preserve

Yield: about 3 cups

Overall, the flavor of fresh watermelon does not preserve well, but if you make pickled watermelon rind and your family flatly refuses to swallow one more juicy bit of the flesh, this recipe is a good way of preserving the surplus.

This preserve features bright red chunks of melon in a pretty, clear jelly with a light, cool flavor.

✄ INGREDIENTS ✄

2 pounds watermelon flesh

3 cups sugar

juice of 1½ lemons

3-ounce pouch liquid pectin

Extract the pink flesh of the watermelon; weigh out 2 pounds. Cut into small cubes, discarding the seeds as you go. Place in a large pot with about 2 cups of cold water, bring to a boil, and cook for 4 minutes. Drain in a colander, then turn out on a clean dish towel to dry further.

Return the watermelon to the pot with the sugar and sprinkle with the lemon juice. Bring slowly to a boil, stirring until all the sugar dissolves. Boil rapidly for 4 minutes. Add one 3-ounce pouch of liquid pectin, return to a boil, and boil rapidly for 2 minutes.

Remove from the heat, skim if necessary, then ladle into hot sterilized jars, leaving ¼-inch headspace. Wipe the rims clean, put the lids in place, and tighten down. Invert the jars for a few minutes, then return to the upright and let cool completely. Check the seals, label, and store in a cool, dry place.

Rose Petal Jam

Yield: about 2 cups

This old-fashioned jam really tastes of the flowers; be sure to use pesticide-free blooms.

✗ INGREDIENTS ✗

2 cups rose petals, tightly packed
(about 24 roses)

2 cups water

2¾ cups sugar

2 tablespoons honey

1 teaspoon lemon juice

Cut the rose petals into strips with scissors, discarding the white base, which is tough. Put the petals in a pan with water; cook for 10 minutes, then lift out and drain, reserving the liquid. Using 1 cup of the liquid obtained, add the sugar and honey and cook until syrupy. Return the rose petals to this syrup and continue to cook gently for about 40 minutes. Add the lemon juice and simmer until set. Depending on the color of the roses used, you may wish to add food coloring to make the jam pink; red roses yield a deep pinkish-red color.

Ladle into hot sterilized jars, leaving ¼-inch headspace. Wipe the rims clean, put the lids in place, and tighten down. Invert the jars for a few minutes, then return to the upright and let cool completely. Check the seals, label, and store in a cool, dry place.

Canteloupe Jam

Yield: about 4 cups

This is the very simplest of jams to make, but the results are surprisingly rewarding. It is clear and bright orange, with an aftertaste of the fresh melon.

✗ INGREDIENTS ✗

2 large cantaloupes

sugar

CANTALOUPE JAM MAKES A DELICIOUS COOKIE TOPPING.

Peel and seed the melons. Chop and sieve, grind, or process the flesh to a pulp. Measure the pulp: for each 2 cups of pulp, add ½ cup of sugar. Put pulp and sugar in a pot over low heat, stirring until the sugar dissolves. Boil briskly at first, then more carefully as the jam boils down, skimming as necessary. Stir occasionally to prevent sticking. When the jam begins to spit, begin testing for set, which may take as long as 45 minutes.

Skim before ladling into hot sterilized jars, leaving ¼-inch headspace. Wipe the rims clean, put the lids in place, and tighten them down. Invert the jars for a few minutes, then return to the upright and let cool completely. Check the seals, label, and store in a cool dry place.

Onion Conserve

Yield: about 4 cups

This is a serious conserve, a sort of chutney that missed its calling: a companion to roast duck, a garnish for dirty rice, a topping for corn bread. It is the perfect condiment for any hearty meal.

✄ INGREDIENTS ✄

1½ pounds onions

2 tablespoons butter

2 tablespoons corn (or other vegetable) oil

1 teaspoon salt

pepper, to taste

1¼ cups sugar

2 apples

1 cup currants

½ cup grenadine

½ cup vinegar

2 cups red wine

Peel the onions and slice very finely. Heat the butter and oil together in a large saucepan. Add the onions, salt, pepper, and sugar. Cover, and cook over low heat, stirring from time to time, until the onions are translucent and tender, about 45 minutes. Do not allow the onions to brown.

Meanwhile, peel, core, and finely grate the apples. When the onions are tender, add the apples, currants, grenadine, vinegar, and red wine. Cook, uncovered, until all the liquid has evaporated and the conserve is thick, about 30 minutes longer, stirring occasionally to prevent sticking.

Skim if necessary and ladle into hot sterilized jars, leaving ¼-inch headspace. Use a nonmetallic spatula to eliminate air bubbles. Wipe the rims clean, put the lids in place, and tighten down. Shake the jars firmly to further eliminate air bubbles. Check the seals, label, and store in a cool, dry place.

ONION CONSERVE

Red Pepper Marmalade

Yield: about 4 cups

This translucent orange-red marmalade is another contestant for the title of "Most Beautiful." The jalapeño here adds a tiny bite without any real heat; the garlic and bay leaf add depth to the flavor without overwhelming the red pepper.

✂ INGREDIENTS ✂

4 large red bell peppers (about 1¼ pounds)

1 jalapeño pepper

1 clove garlic

1½ cups vinegar

1 cup apple juice or cider

½ teaspoon salt

4 bay leaves

juice of 1 lemon

1 package powdered pectin

5 cups sugar

Remember to wear rubber gloves when handling jalapeños, and keep your face out of the steam when cooking them. Keep your fingers away from your face and wash hands thoroughly with soapy water as soon as possible after handling.

Wash all the peppers. Remove the stems, seeds, and internal ribs; cut the bell peppers into strips. Cut the jalapeño into quarters and set aside. Put the bell peppers through a grinder with a medium blade, making sure you catch the juices. Grind the garlic with the red peppers, or chop it finely. Put the ground red peppers and garlic in a large bowl with the jalapeños, vinegar, apple juice, salt, and bay leaves. Cover and let stand overnight in the refrigerator.

The next day, measure out 4 cups of the pepper mixture; combine with the lemon juice and the powdered pectin in a very large pot. Bring rapidly to a boil, stirring constantly. Add the sugar, stirring until dissolved. Return to a rolling boil; at this point, begin timing a 1-minute boil, again stirring constantly. Remove from the heat; skim off any foam, along with the bay leaves and the jalapeño pieces.

Ladle into hot sterilized jars, leaving ¼-inch headspace. Wipe the rims clean, put on the lids, and tighten down. Process for 10 minutes in a boiling water bath; when done, remove the jars from the bath, invert the jars for a few minutes on newspapers or kitchen towels, then return to the upright and let cool completely. Check the seals, label, and store in a cool, dry place.

Peppers can be tricky to jell, sometimes suddenly jelling after a week or so on the shelf in their jars. If this doesn't happen, do not despair: simply return the mixture to the saucepan, bring to a boil, and add lemon juice, half a lemon's worth at a time. Cook between additions and test

RED PEPPER MARMALADE

for set on a saucer. Even when the marmalade tests positively for set, it sometimes takes shelf time before set actually happens. Allow a good 5-minute boil, then repot in newly sterilized jars and follow the above procedure for storage.

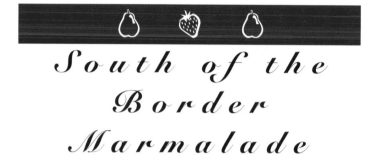

South of the Border Marmalade

Yield: about 3 cups

✂ INGREDIENTS ✂

1¼ pounds tomatillos

1 large green pepper

3 cups sugar

2 jalapeños

6 cloves garlic

1 lemon

2 oranges

1 teaspoon cumin seed

Remember to use rubber gloves when handling jalapeños, and keep your face out of the steam when cooking them. Keep your fingers away from your face and wash hands thoroughly with soapy water as soon as possible after handling chilies.

Remove the papery outer skin and stems of the tomatillos; seed and stem the green pepper. Finely chop the vegetables with a knife; place in a bowl, cover with the sugar, and let stand for a few hours or overnight.

The next morning, transfer the tomatillo mixture to a large saucepan. Stem and seed the jalapeños and finely chop. Peel and chop the garlic cloves, or put through a garlic press. Peel the lemon and 1 orange into pieces large enough to recover later. Remove the pith from all the fruit and discard along with the second orange peel. Slice and chop the flesh of the oranges and lemon. Bruise the cumin seed in a mortar or with the back of a spoon to bring out flavor. Add all of these ingredients to the tomatillo mixture, including the citrus peel. For ease in extracting the peel, you might prefer to tie it in a muslin bag. Bring the contents of the saucepan slowly to a boil, stirring until all the sugar is dissolved. Boil briskly at first, then more gently as the marmalade cooks down and begins to set. When the syrup sheets off a spoon as in a jelly test, remove the saucepan from the heat and remove the orange and lemon peels.

Ladle the marmalade into hot sterilized jars, leaving ¼-inch headspace. Use a nonmetallic spatula to eliminate air bubbles. Wipe the rims clean, put the lids in place, and tighten down. Let cool completely. Check the seals, label, and store in a cool, dry place.

Fennel Preserve

Yield: about 2½ cups

✕ INGREDIENTS ✕

1 large fennel bulb

2 apples

2 cups sugar

2 tablespoons Pernod

Rinse the fennel bulb and trim the base and tops. Chop the entire bulb in small pieces, including the stalks and greens. Peel, core, and chop the apples, tying the peel up in a muslin bag. Put the fennel, apple, and muslin bag in a large saucepan with just enough water to be seen through the top layer. Bring to a boil and simmer until the fennel is tender. Remove the muslin bag; puree the rest of the contents of the saucepan in a blender or food mill. Return the puree to the saucepan and add 2 cups of sugar, stirring until dissolved. Cook carefully until thick, stirring frequently to prevent sticking. This preserve is a "spitter"; to cut down on the clean-up, cover partially as it cooks. When quite thick, remove the pot from the heat and add 2 tablespoons of Pernod, one at a time, stirring after each addition. The alcohol should in large part dissipate, leaving its essence behind to accentuate the natural anise flavor of the fennel. If necessary, cook a few minutes longer to thicken the preserve again.

When ready, ladle into hot sterilized jars, leaving ¼ inch headroom. Use a nonmetallic spatula to eliminate air bubbles. Wipe the rims clean, put the lids in place, and tighten down. Shake each jar gently but firmly to further eliminate air bubbles. When completely cooled, check the seals, label, and store in a cool dry place.

Yellow Tomato Conserve

Yield: about 4 cups

These small, yellow gems, which appear only occasionally in the supermarkets, make a beautiful, sunny jam. It is good in its basic form, but mild enough to spice up with ¼ cup of chopped candied ginger or a cinnamon stick.

✂ INGREDIENTS ✂

2 pounds yellow tomatoes

4 cups sugar

½ cup water

1 lemon

Wash the tomatoes and remove the stem ends, but do not peel or chop. Put the water and sugar in a pot, cooking and stirring to make a syrup. Cut the tomatoes and the lemon into very thin slices and add to the syrup. Cook until thick, about 40 minutes.

Ladle into hot sterilized jars, leaving ¼-inch headspace. Wipe the rims clean, put the lids in place, and tighten down. Invert the jars for a few minutes, then return to the upright and let cool completely. Check the seals, label, and store in a cool, dry place.

YELLOW TOMATO CONSERVE

Tomato-Basil Jam

Yield: about 5 cups

A robust little number: fold it into an omelette at brunch, or serve it as a meat garnish.

✗ INGREDIENTS ✗

6 pounds plum tomatoes

3 lemons

25 basil leaves

3 cups sugar

Scald the tomatoes a few at a time in boiling water; dip them in cold water, then peel. Cut into quarters lengthwise; scoop the juice and seeds into a sieve, straining off the juice with the help of a wooden spoon. Discard the seeds; place the flesh and juice in a large pot, bring slowly to a boil, and simmer 30–45 minutes, reducing the volume by about half. Measure this on the handle of a marked wooden spoon if you wish.

Meanwhile, use a vegetable peeler to remove the outer rind of the lemons in long strips. Tie these into bundles with string and toss them in with the tomatoes. Stir occasionally to prevent sticking.

TOMATO-BASIL JAM

When the tomatoes are sufficiently cooked down, add the sugar, stirring until completely dissolved. Simmer briskly for about 30 minutes, then add the basil and lemon puree, 1 tablespoon at a time until you achieve a balance that suits your taste. Continue to cook, stirring occasionally, about 30 minutes longer.

Ladle into hot sterilized jars, leaving ¼-inch headspace. Eliminate air bubbles with a nonmetallic spatula as necessary. Wipe the rims clean, put the lids in place, and tighten down. Process for 10 minutes in a boiling water bath. Remove and let cool completely. Check the seals, label, and store in a cool, dry place.

Apricot-Zucchini Jam

Yield: about 6 cups

This is a palatable way for the successful gardener to dispose of some of those pounds of zucchini; the apricots are, of course, out of season, so use the dried variety.

APRICOT-ZUCCHINI JAM

✂ INGREDIENTS ✂

½ pound dried apricots

2 pounds prepared zucchini

2 lemons

6 cups sugar

1 cup cranberries (optional)

3 slices ginger root (optional)

Place the apricots in a bowl, cover with cold water, and soak overnight.

In the morning, put the apricots in a saucepan and simmer until tender. While the apricots are cooking, prepare the zucchini: cut off the ends, peel, seed if the zucchini is very large, cut into chunks, and weigh. Boil in a minimal amount of water until tender (or microwave on high in a covered dish for about 10 minutes); mash. Add the zucchini to the cooked apricots, with the grated rind and the juice of 2 lemons and the sugar, stirring until all the sugar dissolves. Boil rapidly for 20–30 minutes; lower the heat as the jam thickens and stir occasionally until set.

If desired, the cranberries, washed and picked over, and the ginger root may be added after the first 20 minutes of boiling. Remove the ginger root before filling the jars.

When ready to set, ladle the jam into hot sterilized jars, leaving ¼-inch headspace. Wipe the rims clean, put the lids in place, and tighten down. Invert the jars for a few minutes, then return to the upright and let cool completely. Check the seals, label, and store in a cool, dry place.

Green Tomato Jelly

Yield: about 2 cups

The color is golden, but the flavor is that of a tomato. A pleasantly surprising jelly, very amenable to the addition of your favorite herbs.

✂ INGREDIENTS ✂

2 pounds green tomatoes

2 cups water
per cup of juice:

1 cup sugar

juice of 1 lemon

Wash the tomatoes; place in a saucepan with the water and simmer, covered, until pulpy—about 1 hour. Strain through a jelly bag; measure the juice obtained, then return it to the saucepan with the juice of 1 lemon and 1 cup of sugar per cup of tomato juice. Stir until the sugar is dissolved and boil rapidly until set (10–15 minutes), stirring occasionally.

Skim as necessary, then ladle into hot sterilized jars, leaving ¼-inch headspace. Wipe the rims clean; put the lids in place, and tighten down. Invert the jars for a few minutes, then return to the upright and let cool completely. Check the seals, label, and store in a cool, dry place.

Carrot Jam

Yield: about 3 cups

✂ INGREDIENTS ✂

1½ pounds carrots

2 cups sugar

1 lemon

½ ounce slivered blanched almonds

1 tablespoon brandy

Wash, peel, and finely chop the carrots; cook in the least possible amount of water until very tender. (This step may be replaced by microwaving the carrots on high in a covered dish until tender, about 10 minutes.) Puree the carrots in a food processor or blender. Return the carrots to the pan, and add the sugar and the juice and grated rind of 1 lemon, stirring until the sugar dissolves. Boil gently until the jam sets, 20–30 minutes, then stir in the thinly slivered almonds and the brandy.

Ladle the jam into hot sterilized jars, leaving ¼-inch headspace. Wipe the rims clean, put the lids in place, and tighten down. Process in a boiling water bath for 10 minutes. Remove from the water bath and invert on racks or clean towels for a few minutes. Return to the upright and let cool completely. Check the seals, label, and store in a cool, dry place.

Note: This jam will not keep without the brandy.

Cucumber Jam

Yield: about 3 cups

✕ INGREDIENTS ✕

2 seedless cucumbers, about 3 pounds

per pound of prepared cucumber:

2 cups sugar

juice of 2 lemons

Peel and dice the cucumbers, then weigh. Put in a pot with a minimal amount of water, just enough to prevent sticking, and cook, covered, until just tender; then for each pound of prepared cucumber add 2 cups of sugar and the juice of 2 lemons. Boil rapidly to set, about 15 minutes. At this point you may wish to add very carefully a drop of green food coloring, though the resulting bright green is far from realistic.

Ladle the jam into hot sterilized jars, leaving ¼-inch headspace. Wipe the rims clean, put the lids in place, and tight-

en down. Invert the jars for a few minutes, then return to the upright and let cool completely. Check the seals, label, and store in a cool, dry place.

Parsley Jelly

Yield: about 2 cups

✕ INGREDIENTS ✕

6 ounces Italian (flat) parsley

per cup of liquid:

juice of 3 lemons

1 cup sugar

Put the parsley and chopped rind of 1 lemon in water just to cover. Bring to a boil and cook, covered, for 1 hour. Strain and measure; return to the pot with the juice of 3 lemons and 1 cup of sugar per cup of liquid. Stir until the sugar dissolves, then boil until nearly set, about 20–30 minutes. Carefully add green food coloring, one drop at a time, until the desired color is achieved. Continue to boil until set, a few minutes longer.

Ladle into hot sterilized jars, leaving ¼-inch headspace. Wipe the rims clean, put the lids in place, and tighten down. Invert the jars for a few minutes, then return to the upright and let cool completely. Check the seals, label, and store in a cool, dry place.

Green Tomato and Orange Conserve

Yield: about 4 cups

This is an excellent way to use up the end-of-season green tomatoes. The amount of oranges used is minimal, so this is much milder than a marmalade. The color is surprising.

✄ INGREDIENTS ✄

4 pounds green tomatoes
5 oranges
10 cups sugar

Wash tomatoes and oranges carefully; remove the stem ends of both, and the seeds of the oranges; grind together rind, peel, and flesh with a coarse blade or coarsely chop in the food processor. Put in a pot with the sugar and bring to a boil, stirring until the sugar dissolves. Boil until thick and clear, about 45 minutes.

Ladle into hot sterilized jars, leaving ¼-inch headspace. Wipe the rims clean at once, but cool before putting the lids in place and tightening down. Process in a boiling water bath for 15 minutes; remove from the water bath and invert for a few minutes, then return to the upright and let cool completely. Check the seals, label, and store in a cool, dry place.

Rutabaga and Cranberry Conserve

Yield: about 4 cups

At our house, the rutabaga has an honored place on the Thanksgiving table—to remind us how good the rest of the feast is (actually, some of us like it). This conserve is a concession to those of us who don't like the bitterness of the rutabaga, most of which is removed by the brandy.

> ✄ I N G R E D I E N T S ✄
>
> 2 rutabagas (about 2 pounds)
>
> 4 cups sugar
>
> 2 lemons
>
> 1 stick cinnamon
>
> ¼ teaspoon ground cloves
>
> 1 cup dried cranberries
>
> 2 tablespoons brandy or bourbon
>
> ½ cup broken walnuts (optional)

Peel the rutabagas and cut in large chunks to speed the cooking time. Boil covered in water just to cover until tender, about 30–40 minutes; drain well and puree in a food processor or blender. Return to the pot and add the sugar, the juice of 2 lemons and the grated rind of 1 lemon, the spices, and the cranberries. Cook until thick, about 15–20 minutes; add the walnuts, if desired, and the brandy and return to a boil briefly.

Ladle into sterilized jars, leaving ¼-inch headspace. Wipe the rims clean, put the lids in place, and tighten down. Process in a boiling water bath for 10 minutes. Remove and let cool completely. Check the seals, label, and store in a cool, dry place.

Pumpkin (or Squash) Jam

Yield: about 3½ cups

Pumpkins are with us only briefly in the fall; winter squashes are available for months on end. This recipe is equally successful using pumpkin or an orange squash such as butternut. You might be tempted to use brown sugar for its richer flavor; be warned that your product will be dark brown instead of orange.

> ✄ I N G R E D I E N T S ✄
>
> 2 pounds of pumpkin or winter squash
>
> 2 small lemons
>
> spices: to taste (a few slices of ginger root, or 4–5 cloves, or a cinnamon stick, or ½ teaspoon of your favorite spice)
>
> 4 cups sugar

Peel, seed, cube, and weigh the pumpkin. Boil until tender and drain well. (You may microwave the prepared pumpkin on high in a covered dish until tender, about 12 minutes.) Mash and place in a pan with the grated rind and juice of the lemons and your chosen spices. Bring gently to a boil; add the sugar, stirring until dissolved. Boil gently until thick, about 20 minutes.

If you have used whole spices, skim them off before ladling into hot sterilized jars, leaving ¼-inch headspace. Wipe the rims clean, put the lids in place, and tighten down. Invert the jars for a few minutes, then return to the upright and let cool completely. Check the seals, label, and store in a cool, dry place.

Zucchini Cream

Yield: about 3 cups

The flavor of this delicious preserve is strong and lemony, with the texture of a stiff puree or butter.

✄ INGREDIENTS ✄

2 pounds zucchini
2 cups sugar
½ cup butter
2 lemons

Cut off stem and blossom ends of the zucchini and peel. If the zucchini are very large, cut in half lengthwise and remove the seeds. If small, leave whole. Boil in water until tender. (Or you may cook by microwaving on high in a covered dish until tender, about 10 minutes.) In either case, drain well, then process in a blender or mash to a smooth pulp. Cook in the top of a double boiler over hot water with the sugar, the butter, and the juice and grated rind of the lemons, stirring frequently until thick and creamy, about 15 minutes.

Ladle into hot sterilized jars, leaving ¼-inch headspace. Wipe the rims clean, put the lids in place, and tighten down. Invert the jars for a few minutes, then return to the upright and let cool completely. Check the seals, label, and store in a cool, dry place.

Garlic-Herb Marmalade

Yield: about 4 cups

You may use as much or as little garlic as you like for this unusual preserve. A dozen cloves make for a very strong flavor. Use it as a meat garnish or cocktail accompaniment.

GARLIC-HERB MARMALADE IS PERFECTLY AT HOME ON A PLATTER OF APPETIZERS.

✂ INGREDIENTS ✂

10–12 cloves garlic

fresh herbs: parsley, sage, basil, rosemary, thyme, etc.

½ cup white wine vinegar

1½ cups white wine

juice of 1 lemon

3¼ cups sugar

6-ounce bottle liquid pectin (2 pouches)

Chop the garlic very finely with a knife, or process in a blender. Rinse the herbs thoroughly and tie in a bundle. Set aside a teaspoonful of the garlic; place the rest in a saucepan with a small amount of water (1 cup) and the bundle of herbs. Boil over moderate heat for 15 minutes.

Remove the herb bundle, leaving in the liquid any escaped thyme leaves, if you have used them. Transfer the liquid to a large glass measuring cup. Add ½ cup white wine vinegar, and however much white wine is necessary to bring the amount of liquid to 2 cups. Return the liquid to a very large saucepan. Add the lemon juice and the sugar, stirring until the sugar dissolves. Bring to a full boil; add the reserved garlic and the liquid pectin. Return to a rolling boil, let boil for 1 minute, then remove from the heat. Skim off the foam.

Let cool until the marmalade begins to thicken: this will allow the bits of garlic to remain in suspension. Stir before pouring into hot sterilized jars, leaving ¼-inch headspace. Wipe the rims clean, put the lids in place, and tighten down. Invert the jars for a few minutes to complete the seal, then return to the upright and let cool completely. Check the seals, label, and store in a cool, dry place.

Horseradish Jelly

Yield: about 3 cups

This is an old family recipe from the Pittsburgh area. Originally intended as a molded garnish for roast beef or chicken, it yields a very stiff jelly.

✂ INGREDIENTS ✂

½ cup prepared horseradish, fresh or with as few additives as possible

½ cup cider vinegar

3¼ cups sugar

½ cup liquid pectin

To prepare fresh horse radish, peel and grate with a fine blade.

In a large saucepan, heat and stir the sugar, horseradish, and vinegar until the sugar dissolves. Bring to a boil, then stir in the pectin all at once. Bring back to a full rolling boil, stirring constantly. Remove from the heat and skim off the foam.

Pour into hot sterilized jars, leaving ¼-inch headspace. Wipe the rims clean, put the lids in place, and tighten down. Invert the jars for a few minutes, then return to the upright and let cool completely. Check the seals, label, and store in a cool, dry place.

Jalapeño Jelly

Yield: about 7 cups

This is a hot gift item, but the recipient must have either an adventuresome palate or a sense of humor. The jelly is a great accompaniment for meats, instead of the traditional mint jelly, for instance. Or serve it on cream cheese and crackers.

✂ INGREDIENTS ✂

1½ cups green bell pepper

8–10 jalapeño peppers

1½ cups cider vinegar

6½ cups granulated sugar

6 ounces liquid pectin

2 drops green food coloring

Remember to wear rubber gloves when handling jalapeños, and keep your face out of the steam when cooking them. Keep your fingers away from your face and wash hands thoroughly with soapy water as soon as possible after handling.

Wash all the peppers. Remove the seeds and inner white flesh of the bell peppers. Remove the caps from the jalapeños, but do not seed. Put all the peppers through a food grinder or process, without pureeing too finely, in the blender. Mix the peppers, vinegar, and sugar in a large pan and bring to a rolling boil. Add the liquid pectin, then return to a rolling boil. Cook for 1 minute, stirring constantly. Remove from the burner and let settle for a few minutes, then skim off any foam. Carefully add the food coloring, if desired, a drop at a time.

Ladle into hot sterilized jars, leaving ¼-inch headspace. Wipe the rims clean, put the lids in place, and tighten down. Invert the jars for a few minutes, then return to the upright and let cool completely. Check the seals, label, and store in a cool, dry place.

Field and Stream

Uncle Joe Garritee's Violet Jelly

Yield: about 4 cups

Our friend Cisco used to help his uncle pick violets for this jelly and later watch the juice turn midnight blue, then crimson. Uncle Joe's mother had the recipe from her mother. They believed the blossoms to be high in vitamin C.

✗ INGREDIENTS ✗

1 pint violets
1 package commercial pectin powder
juice of 1 lemon
4 cups sugar

Fill a pint jar with violet flower heads (no stems), firmly packed but not squashed or bruised. Pour very hot water to cover the flowers, put the lid on the jar, and let sit for 24 hours. If the flowers do not remain submerged after an hour or so, add enough water to keep them down.

After 24 hours, strain, reserving the liquid and discarding the violets. Put 2 cups of the liquid in a pan and stir in 1 package of commercial pectin powder and the lemon juice; bring to a boil. Add 4 cups of sugar, stirring until dissolved. Return to a boil and boil rapidly for 1 minute, stirring constantly.

Remove from the heat, skim, and pour into hot sterilized jars, leaving ¼-inch headspace. Wipe the rims clean, put the lids in place, and seal. Invert the jars for a few minutes, then return to the upright and let cool completely. Check the seals, label, and store in a cool, dry place.

Old-time French Strawberry Preserve

Yield: about 5 cups

This recipe was meant to be made with what the French call "jam sugar," which is not readily available in the United States and Canada. It is adapted here by the addition of lemon juice and a lot of extra cooking time, but it is still delicious.

✂ INGREDIENTS ✂

2 pounds strawberries (2 quarts)

4 cups sugar

peel of 1 orange, in one long strip, if possible

juice of 1 lemon

2 tablespoons Cointreau

Wash the berries and drain as dry as possible. Remove the stems and caps; cut into small pieces. Mix in a bowl with the sugar and orange peel, and let stand overnight.

In the morning, transfer to a large pot, stirring over low heat until the sugar is dissolved. Add the lemon juice and cook until set, about 30–40 minutes. Remove from the heat and skim off the foam before adding the Cointreau, a tablespoon at a time. Ladle into hot sterilized jars, leaving ¼-inch headspace. Wipe the rims clean, put the lids in place, and tighten down. Invert the jars for a few minutes, then return to the upright and let cool completely. Check the seals, label, and store in a cool, dry place.

Persimmon Jam

Yield: about 4 cups

You are more likely to find the Asian persimmon at your local grocery than the native variety. Yellow to red in color, slightly heart-shaped, 2-3 inches in diameter, the Asian persimmon is grown commercially in this country, whereas its smaller American cousin is not. The latter flourishes in the wild as far north as Pennsylvania, however. Before use, either variety must be "soft-ripe," when it loses its youthful astringency.

✂ INGREDIENTS ✂

2 pounds persimmons (about 6)

juice of 1 lemon

3 cups sugar

1-inch piece of vanilla bean

1 apple

Wash the persimmons; remove the stem and calyx. If the skin is tough, peel. Remove the seeds, and put the flesh through a grinder or chop finely. Sprinkle with the lemon juice and the sugar. Let stand covered in a bowl to juice up, 2–3 hours or overnight.

Transfer the persimmons and their juices to a large pan; add the piece of vanilla bean and the apple, peeled (in one long piece, if possible), cored, and chopped. Add the piece of apple peel for additional pectin. Bring to a boil, stirring until all the sugar is dissolved. Boil briskly at first, then more gently, stirring frequently to avoid sticking. In about 30 minutes, when ready to set, remove the apple peel and the vanilla bean.

Ladle into hot sterilized jars, leaving ¼-inch headspace. Wipe the rims clean, put the lids in place, and tighten down. Invert the jars for a few minutes, then return to the upright and let cool completely. Check the seals, label, and store in a cool, dry place.

PERSIMMON JAM

Strawberry Preserve

Yield: about 3½ cups

✄ INGREDIENTS ✄

2 pounds strawberries (2 quarts)

2 cups sugar

1 apple

Wash the berries gently and drain as dry as possible. Remove the stems and caps; cut the smaller berries in half and the larger into quarters. Place in a bowl, cover with the sugar, and let stand a few hours or overnight to juice up.

Transfer the berries to a pot with the apple, which has been peeled, cored, and grated. Bring slowly to a boil and cook for 15 minutes, occasionally dragging a wooden spoon across the bottom of the pot to make sure the jam is not sticking. Scoop out the berries with a slotted spoon and set aside. Cook the syrup briskly for about 15 minutes to reduce it, then add the lemon juice and return the berries to the pot. Continue to cook until set.

Ladle into hot sterilized jars, leaving ¼-inch headspace. Wipe the rims clean, put the lids in place, and tighten down. Invert the jars for a few minutes, then return to the upright and let cool completely. Check the seals, label, and store in a cool, dry place.

STRAWBERRY PRESERVE

Spicy Cranberry Conserve

Yield: about 5 cups

This preserve is sweeter than the cranberry sauce that usually accompanies the holiday turkey. However, it keeps better without refrigeration than low-sugar cranberry sauce, and will substitute nicely in a pinch.

✵ INGREDIENTS ✵

1 pound cranberries (1 quart)

1 cup fruit juice (apple, pineapple, or white grape)

1 stick cinnamon

¼ teaspoon fennel seed

2 whole cloves (or ¼ teaspoon ground clove)

½ teaspoon ground allspice

1 orange

½ cup raisins

3 cups sugar

1 cup broken walnuts (optional)

Rinse the berries and pick over them for bruising and stems. Heat in 1 cup fruit juice until they burst; let boil for 5 minutes or so. Bruise the fennel seed and the allspice and tie all the spices into a muslin bag. Add to the cranberries at once.

Wash the orange, slice it finely, seed, and then chop it; add it to the cranberries with the raisins. Add the sugar slowly, stirring until completely dissolved. Boil for 10 minutes before adding the walnuts, if desired; then continue boiling until set, but no more than 20 minutes. Stir occasionally to prevent sticking. Remove from the heat and let stand for 5 minutes before removing the spice bag. If you have opted for walnuts, let cool partially so the nuts don't float to the top.

Ladle into hot sterilized jars, leaving ¼-inch headspace. Wipe the rims clean, put the lids in place, and tighten down. Invert the jars for a few minutes to complete the seal, then return to the upright and let cool completely. Check the seals, label, and store in a cool, dry place.

SPICY CRANBERRY CONSERVE MAKES A DELICIOUS AND FEISTY ACCOMPANIMENT FOR GAME BIRDS SUCH AS CORNISH HEN.

Blueberry Jam

Yield: about 6 cups ~8

✗ INGREDIENTS ✗

3 pounds blueberries

¼ cup water

1–2 sticks cinnamon

grating of nutmeg (optional) ⅛ t.

4 cups sugar

juice of 1 lemon (medium)

Wash and pick over the blueberries; crush a few in the bottom of the pot. Add the water and spices; boil together gently until the berries have burst. Stir in the sugar and the lemon juice until dissolved. Boil gently until the jam sets, about 20 minutes longer.

Ladle into hot sterilized jars, leaving ¼-inch headspace. Wipe the rims clean, put the lids in place, and tighten down. Invert the jars for a few minutes to complete the seal, then return to the upright and let cool completely. Check the seals, label, and store in a cool, dry place.

Chestnut Spread

Yield: about 4 cups

✗ INGREDIENTS ✗

2 pounds chestnuts

1 cup water

3 cups sugar

2-inch piece of vanilla bean (or 2 teaspoons vanilla extract)

½ cup cognac (optional)

If you are using dried chestnuts, soak in fresh water overnight to reconstitute.

Score the reconstituted or fresh chestnuts top and bottom with a sharp knife. Boil in water to cover for 10–20 minutes (this will allow you to peel the chestnuts). Be sure to peel the dark inner skin too as it is quite bitter.

After peeling the chestnuts, cover them with fresh water and boil until tender. Process in the blender or food processor to a puree.

In a pot, make a syrup of the water, sugar, and vanilla; add the chestnuts and cook gently until thick. At this point you may add ½ cup cognac, if desired.

Ladle into hot sterilized jars, leaving ¼-inch headspace. Wipe the rims clean, put the lids in place, and tighten down. Process 20 minutes in a boiling water bath. Remove from the water bath and let cool completely. Check the seals, label and store in as dry a place as possible. This spread does not keep very well, probably no more than 3 months, but may be frozen or refrigerated to prolong its life. Do not count on the normal shelf life of one year.

until set, stirring frequently to prevent sticking, about 30 minutes. When the jam has set, remove the apple peel.

Ladle the jam into hot sterilized jars, leaving ¼-inch headspace. Wipe the rims clean, put the lids in place, and tighten down. Invert the jars for a few minutes to complete the seal, then return to the upright and let cool completely. Check the seals, label, and store in a cool, dry place.

Raspberry Jam

Yield: about 6 cups

✄ INGREDIENTS ✄

2 pounds red raspberries

2 apples

6 cups sugar

Wash and pick over the raspberries; place in a large pot over very low heat. Peel (reserving a few long pieces of the peel), quarter, and core the apples. Grate the quarters or chop very finely and add to the raspberries. Add the peel, if possible: raspberries are low in pectin. Simmer the fruits gently for 5 minutes before gradually stirring in the sugar. Cook gently

Four-Berry Jam

Yield: about 6 cups

To my New England soul, this delicious jam makes extravagant use of berries. The proportions of the fruits are variable, but basically, the strawberries are the filler, or vehicle, for the others.

✂ INGREDIENTS ✂

1 pound strawberries

4 cups sugar (or, 1 cup sugar per cup of berries)

½ pound blueberries

6 ounces blackberries

6 ounces raspberries

juice of 1 lemon

Wash and stem the strawberries; cut the larger ones in half. Crush a few in the bottom of the saucepan, toss in the rest, and add half the sugar (2 cups). Heat very slowly over low heat to release the juices, stirring carefully to prevent sticking.

Wash and pick over the blueberries, blackberries, and raspberries. When the strawberries have come to a boil and simmered for 5 minutes, add the other berries, the lemon juice, and the rest of the sugar. Return to a boil, stirring until all the sugar is dissolved. Cook for 10 minutes; scoop out most of the berries with a slotted spoon, but continue to cook down the juices for a further 10 minutes. Return the berries to the pot and continue to cook until set, about 10–15 minutes.

Ladle into hot sterilized jars, leaving ¼-inch headspace. Wipe the rims clean, put the lids in place, and tighten down. Invert the jars for a few minutes to complete the seal, then return to the upright and let cool completely. Check the seals, label, and store in a cool, dry place.

FOUR-BERRY JAM IS PERHAPS THE ULTIMATE CROWD-PLEASER.

Exotica

Coconut Jam

Yield: about 4 cups (per pound of coconut meat)

In this recipe, pectin is replaced as a jelling agent by egg yolks. The preserve will keep for about 6 months if carefully stored in a cool, dark, dry place.

✗ INGREDIENTS ✗

fresh coconut, or unsweetened, grated frozen coconut (1 fresh coconut will yield 1 pound of prepared meat)

per pound of coconut meat:

2 cups sugar

½ cup water

½ of a vanilla bean

2 egg yolks

If you are using fresh coconuts, punch holes in the "eyes" and drain the milk into a bowl. Break open the outer shell and discard. Using a vegetable peeler, peel off the inner brown skin. Weigh the meat; process with a fine grater.

Make a syrup by briefly boiling the sugar and water together. Add the vanilla bean, the coconut milk, and, lastly, the coconut meat. Cook very carefully over low heat until the coconut is translucent, stirring and adding water as necessary to prevent scorching. This may take up to an hour or more.

Beat the egg yolks with 2 teaspoons of warm water. Dribble this mixture slowly into the coconut, stirring carefully at the very point of entry to avoid scrambling the eggs: if they scramble they will no longer serve to bind the jam.

Remove the vanilla bean, and ladle the jam into hot sterilized jars, leaving ¼-inch headspace. Use a nonmetallic spatula to help remove air bubbles. Wipe the rims clean, put the lids in place, and tighten down. Shake the jars firmly to remove any remaining air bubbles. Let cool completely. Check the seals, label, and store in a cool, dry, and dark place. Make sure the label bears the 6-month expiration date.

Ginger Marmalade

Yield: about 4 cups

✂ INGREDIENTS ✂

3 pounds tart apples

2 cups water

8 ounces Canton ginger

sugar

Wash the apples and chop coarsely without peeling or coring. Simmer in the water until very pulpy. Strain through a jelly bag overnight.

In the morning, measure the juice together with the ginger, finely chopped. Put in a pan with 1 cup of sugar per cup of juice and ginger combined; bring slowly to a boil, stirring until the sugar is dissolved. Boil rapidly until set, about 10 minutes.

Remove from the heat, ladle into hot sterilized jars, leaving ¼-inch headspace. Wipe the rims clean, put the lids in place, and tighten down. Invert the jars for a few moments, then return to the upright, shake firmly to bring air bubbles back to the top, and let cool completely. Check the seals, label, and store in a cool, dry place.

GINGER MARMALADE MAKES AN EXCELLENT DIPPING SAUCE FOR SHRIMP TEMPURA.

Banana Jam

Yield: about 4 cups

✂ INGREDIENTS ✂

2 pounds bananas

1-inch piece of vanilla bean

juice of 4 oranges

juice of 4 lemons

3 cups sugar

Peel and slice the bananas. Place in a saucepan with the vanilla bean and the juice of the oranges and lemons (together these should measure about 3 cups). Add the sugar, stirring until dissolved, and bring slowly to a boil. Cook over low heat, stirring occasionally at first, and more frequently as the jam thickens. When quite thick, after about 30 minutes, skim if necessary, removing the piece of vanilla bean.

Ladle into hot sterilized jars, leaving ¼-inch headspace. Wipe the rims clean, put the lids in place, and tighten down. Invert the jars for a few minutes, then return to the upright and let cool completely. Check the seals, label, and store in a cool, dry place.

Plantain Jam

Yield: about 8 cups

The texture, moisture content, and flavor of plantains differ from the common banana. This hearty jam is slightly grainy, and lacks a pronounced banana flavor, but the rum and cloves give it a good tropical punch.

✄ INGREDIENTS ✄

2 pounds plantain bananas

6 cloves

juice of 4 lemons

juice of 4 oranges

3 cups sugar

¼ cup dark rum

Peel and slice the bananas. Place in a saucepan with the cloves and the juice of the lemons and oranges (about 3 cups altogether). Add the sugar, stirring until dissolved, and bring slowly to a boil. Cook over low heat until thick, stirring occasionally to prevent sticking. When quite thick, stir in the rum; continue to cook a few minutes longer. You may remove the cloves or not, as you wish.

Ladle the jam into hot sterilized jars, leaving ¼-inch head-space. Wipe the rims clean, put the lids in place, and tighten down. Invert the jars for a few minutes, then return to the upright. As this is a thick jam, shake the jars gently but firmly to make sure the air bubbles are all out. Let cool completely. Check the seals, label, and store in a cool, dry place.

Pepino Jam

Yield: about 8 cups

This is an exotic melon that is entirely edible except for its paper-thin skin.

✄ INGREDIENTS ✄

3 pounds pepinos (7 or 8 largish melons)

juice of 2 lemons

1½ cups sugar

Peel the melons and cut in chunks. Bring gently to a boil in a minimum of water (¼ cup). Continue to simmer until very soft, about 20 minutes. When soft, add the lemon juice and the sugar, stirring until completely dissolved. Boil until thick, about 15 minutes longer, stirring frequently at the end of the cooking to prevent sticking. Skim if necessary.

Ladle into hot sterilized jars, leaving ¼-inch headspace. Wipe the rims clean, put the lids in place, and tighten down. Invert the jars for a few minutes, then return to the upright and let cool completely. Check the seals, label, and store in a cool, dry place.

PEPINOS

Guava Jelly

Yield: about 5 cups

✶ INGREDIENTS ✶

24 guavas

¼ cup lemon juice

sugar: 1 cup per cup of juice (you will need about 4 cups for this recipe)

Wash and quarter the guavas. Place in a saucepan with water just to cover. Bring to a boil and simmer, covered, about 30 minutes, or until the guavas are very tender. Strain through a jelly bag for several hours or overnight. Do not squeeze the bag: not only will the juice be cloudy, but it will be bitter as well.

Measure the juice obtained; transfer to a saucepan and bring to a boil. Cook for 5 minutes, then add the lemon juice and 1 cup of sugar per cup of juice. Do not process more than 4 cups of juice at a time. Stir until all the sugar is dissolved, then boil rapidly until set. This should take about 20 minutes, though the time is extremely variable.

Pour into hot sterilized jars, leaving ¼-inch headspace. Wipe the rims clean, put the lids in place, and tighten down. Invert the jars for a few minutes to vacuum seal, then return to the upright and let cool completely. Check the seals, label, and store in a cool, dry place.

Fresh Fig Preserve

Yield: about 4 cups

This preserve is so very mild that you may want to add ½ teaspoon of your favorite spices, but you will then lose the fig flavor.

✗ INGREDIENTS ✗

2 pounds ripe figs (about 24)

4 cups sugar

juice of 2 lemons

FRESH FIGS

Wash, stem, and quarter the figs. Place in a saucepan with the lemon juice and the sugar. Stir over moderate heat until all the sugar is dissolved. Bring slowly to a boil, then let boil rapidly until set. This jam is surprisingly quick to set; it will be ready to pot in about 20 minutes.

Skim; ladle into hot sterilized jars, leaving ¼-inch headspace. Wipe the rims clean, put the lids in place, and tighten down. Invert the jars for a few minutes to vacuum seal, then return to the upright and let cool completely. Check the seals, label, and store in a cool, dry place.

Preserved (Canton) Ginger

Yield: about 4 cups

This is a long, but not difficult, process. It has four stages, each of which must be left to stand for several hours, or overnight.

It yields a ginger for use in jams and marmalades that retains its savor but will not overwhelm either your taste buds or the flavor of the other ingredients.

✂ I N G R E D I E N T S ✂

1¼ pounds ginger root

3 cups sugar

1 lemon

1 cup light corn syrup

Peel the ginger root and cut it into slices about ¼-inch thick. Place in a large stainless steel or other nonreactive saucepan and cover with 2 inches of water. Bring slowly to a boil and cook gently for about 45 minutes, until tender. Stir in 1 cup sugar, stirring until dissolved. Bring to a boil, remove from the heat, and let stand, covered, several hours or overnight.

Return the ginger and sugar mixture to a boil, simmer 15 minutes, then add 1 lemon, thinly sliced, and the corn syrup. Simmer 15 minutes longer, stirring occasionally. Again, remove from the heat and let stand, covered, several hours or overnight.

Bring mixture back to a boil and stir in 1 cup sugar. Cook gently for 30 minutes, stirring frequently. Add 1 more cup sugar, stirring until dissolved. Remove from the heat, cover, and let stand as before, for several hours or overnight.

Carefully bring the mixture to a boil and cook until the ginger is translucent and the syrup thick, about 30 minutes, stirring very often to prevent scorching.

Store in sterile pint jars, leaving ¼-inch headspace. Wipe the rims clean, put the lids in place, and tighten down. Invert for 10 minutes, then return to the upright. Let cool completely, check the seals, and label. Store in a cool, dry place.

Crystallized Ginger

Yield: about 4 cups

This is a further evolution of the above recipe for Canton Ginger.

When you have finished the fourth cooking above, drain the ginger and dry on racks overnight. When quite dry, roll in granulated sugar. Store in glass jars. The syrup may be used as a spicy sauce, or as flavoring in other sauces, jams, and marmalades.

Feijoa Jelly

Yield: about 4 cups

The feijoa is also known as the pineapple guava; it looks very much like its guava cousin, though smaller, and it makes a very different jelly.

✄ INGREDIENTS ✄

1 pound feijoas
per cup of juice:
1 tablespoon lemon juice
1¼ cups sugar (you will need 3–4 cups for this recipe)

Wash and quarter the feijoas. Place in a saucepan with water just to cover and boil, covered, about 30 minutes, or until the fruit is very tender. Strain through a jelly bag for several hours or overnight. The juice is of a rather unpleasant gray color, but do not be discouraged.

Measure the juice obtained—there should be about 3 cups. Transfer to a large saucepan, bring to a boil and cook for 5 minutes. For each cup of juice, stir in 1 tablespoon of lemon juice

FEIJOA JELLY IS AN EXCELLENT TOPPING FOR TOAST.

and 1¼ cups of sugar. Boil rapidly until set (about 15 minutes), remove from the heat, and skim. You will perceive a decided pineapple flavor, and a jelly that has gone from gray to golden.

Pour into hot sterilized jars, leaving ¼-inch headspace. Wipe the rims clean, put the lids in place, and tighten down. Invert the jars for a few minutes to vacuum seal, then return to the upright and let cool completely. Check the seals, label, and store in a cool, dry place.

Cherimoya Jam

Yield: about 4 cups

This is a dull green exotic fruit, the size of a large, vaguely heart-shaped mango. Its flesh is white and refreshing with a slightly bitter aftertaste. There is an internal stem, randomly surrounded by large black seeds in edible sacs.

✄ INGREDIENTS ✄

2 cherimoyas (about 2 pounds)
juice of 2 lemons
3½ cups sugar
½ teaspoon ground cardamom (optional)

Cut the cherimoyas in half; remove the internal stem and as many seeds as are readily accessible (the rest will float free in the cooking). Place the flesh in a bowl, sprinkle with the lemon juice and the sugar. Let stand for an hour to juice up, then put in a pot, add the cardamom, if desired, bring gently to a boil, and simmer to set, about 30 minutes.

Skim off any remaining seeds before ladling the jam into hot sterilized jars, leaving ¼-inch headspace. Wipe the rims clean, put the lids in place, and tighten down. Invert the jars for a few minutes, then return to the upright and let cool completely. Check the seals, label, and store in a cool, dry place.

Cactus Pear Butter

Yield: about 3 cups

The preparation of the fruit for this recipe is rather more involved than most as it requires two separate cooking stages for the pears; your reward for the extra work is a smooth, honeyed spread.

✄ I N G R E D I E N T S ✄

1 pound cactus pears (prickly pears)

1 pound tart apples (Green MacIntosh or Granny Smith)

¾ cup honey

Peel the cactus pears and cut them in half. Scoop out the center pulp containing the seeds and cook this pulp in a small amount of water until the seeds are loosened. Push the pulp through a sieve, reserving the juice and discarding the seeds.

Cut the remaining outer pulp of the pears into pieces. Peel and core the apples; cut into small chunks. Put the apples and the outer pulp of the pears in a pot with the juice obtained from the inner pulp and a small amount of water. Cook until the fruits are quite tender, about 30–40 minutes. Add the honey and sugar, stirring until completely dissolved. Boil rapidly to set, another 15–20 minutes.

Ladle the butter into hot sterilized jars, leaving ¼-inch headspace. Wipe the rims clean, put the lids in place, and tighten down. Invert the jars for a few minutes, then return to the upright and let cool completely. Check the seals, label, and store in a cool, dry place.

Kiwano (Horned Melon) Jelly

Yield: about 2 cups

This bright yellow fruit from New Zealand is oval in shape, weighs about ½ pound, and is covered all over with pointy (but not sharp) projections, its horns. The inside is bright watery green, and full of cantaloupe-type seeds. It is tart and refreshing.

✗ INGREDIENTS ✗

2 pounds kiwanos (about 4)

sugar

Wash the fruit as best you can, cut it into quarters, and boil in water to cover, until the skin is soft, about 30–40 minutes. Strain through a jelly bag overnight; the juice is particularly viscous.

In the morning measure the juice obtained. Put it in a pot, bring to a boil and boil for 5 minutes. Add ¾ cup of sugar for each cup of juice, stirring until dissolved. Boil until set, about 30 minutes.

Ladle into hot sterilized jars, leaving ¼-inch headspace. Wipe the rims clean, put the lids in place, and tighten down. Invert the jars for a few minutes, return to the upright and let cool completely. Check the seals, label, and store in a cool, dry place.

ABOVE: KIWANO (HORNED MELON)
OPPOSITE: KIWANO JELLY

Mango Jam

Yield: about 6 cups

✄ INGREDIENTS ✄

4 pounds slightly underripe, firm mangoes

6 cups sugar

2 lemons

1 tablespoon butter

Peel the mangoes, cut into pieces, and discard the pits. Put in a bowl; cover with the sugar and let stand 2 hours to juice up. At the end of that time, transfer to a pot, and add the grated rind of the lemons and their pulp sliced very thinly. Discard the pith of the lemons. Stir the fruit while it comes to a boil, until the sugar is dissolved, then cook 1½ hours over low heat until set, stirring occasionally to prevent sticking. Skim off any foam; add the tablespoon of butter and stir in to eliminate the last traces of foam.

Ladle into hot sterilized jars, leaving ¼-inch headspace. Wipe the rims clean, put the lids in place, and tighten down. Invert the jars for a few minutes, then return to the upright and let cool completely. Check the seals, label, and store in a cool, dry place.

Orange-Papaya Conserve

Yield: about 4 cups

This is a complicated recipe, but the results are quite exotic, both in looks and taste.

✄ INGREDIENTS ✄

2 pounds papayas

6 cups sugar

2 pounds oranges

juice of 2 lemons

Peel, seed, and cube the papayas. Place in a bowl with half the sugar (3 cups) to juice up.

While waiting, prepare the oranges: remove the outer peel of 1 orange in as few pieces as possible (you will have to remove it later) and discard the pith of this orange, along with the peel and pith of all the others. Separate all the segments, keeping them as intact as possible. Barely cover the segments with boiling water and let stand 5 minutes. Drain; remove the pips by spearing with a sewing needle, making the fewest and smallest holes possible. Put the remaining half of the sugar (3 cups) in a pan with 2 cups of water and bring to a boil, stirring until the sugar dissolves. Add the orange segments. Cook 45 minutes over medium heat.

By now the papaya is ready to be cooked. Put it in another pan and bring to a boil, stirring until the sugar is dissolved. Cook very gently for 1½ hours, stirring occasionally to prevent sticking.

When the papaya is about ready to set, remove the peel from the orange mixture, combine the two mixtures, and add the juice of 2 lemons to aid the setting. Cook about 5 minutes more.

Ladle carefully into hot sterilized jars, leaving ¼–inch headspace. Wipe the rims clean, put the lids in place, and tighten down. Invert the jars for a few minutes, then return to the upright and let cool completely. Check the seals, label, and store in a cool, dry place.

Pineapple Carambola Jam

Yield: about 4 cups

✂ INGREDIENTS ✂

1 large pineapple

juice of 3 lemons

6 cups sugar

6 star fruits (carambolas)

Peel the pineapple, remove the eyes, and core. Crush the flesh by putting it through a grinder. Put in a pan with the juice of the lemons and the sugar; bring to a boil, stirring until the sugar dissolves. Boil rapidly for 15 minutes.

Wash the carambolas; cut crosswise into ¼-inch slices, removing the seeds, if any. When the pineapple has boiled for 15 minutes, add the carambola slices and cook for 15 minutes longer, stirring occasionally to prevent sticking. If this is done gently the carambolas will retain their star shape.

When the jam sets, ladle into hot sterilized jars, leaving ¼-inch headspace. Wipe the rims clean, put the lids in place, and tighten down. Invert the jars for a few minutes, then return to the upright and let cool completely. Check the seals, label, and store in a cool, dry place.

Pineapple Jam

Yield: about 4 cups

✂ INGREDIENTS ✂

4 pounds pineapple (1 large or 2 medium)

3 cups water

4 cups sugar

Peel the pineapples, core, and remove the eyes. Chop finely or put through a grinder with a coarse blade. If the pineapple is extremely ripe, do this on a plate to catch the juice.

Boil the water and stir in the sugar to make a syrup. Add the crushed pineapple and boil to set, about 15–20 minutes.

Ladle into hot sterilized jars, leaving ¼-inch headspace. Wipe the rims clean, put the lids in place, and tighten down. Invert the jars for a few minutes, then return to the upright and let cool completely. Check the seals, label, and store in a cool, dry place.

Put the pineapple juice, lemon juice, and the sugar into a large pan, stirring over low heat until the sugar dissolves. Bring to a rolling boil and add the pectin. Continue to boil for another minute, then remove from the heat.

Put into hot sterilized jars, leaving ¼-inch headspace. Wipe the rims clean, put the lids in place, and tighten down. Invert the jars for a few minutes, then return to the upright and let cool completely. Check the seals, label, and store in a cool, dry place.

Pineapple Jelly

Yield: about 4½ cups

This is a mild jelly that is a good candidate for sprigs of fresh herbs; try rosemary, sage, or chives.

✄ INGREDIENTS ✄

4 cups canned pineapple juice
juice of 2 lemons
4 cups sugar
2 pouches liquid pectin (6 ounces)

Spiced Pineapple-Pear Jam

Yield: about 4½ cups

✄ INGREDIENTS ✄

2 pounds pears
1 pineapple
1 small lemon
1 small orange
4 cups sugar
3 cloves
1 stick cinnamon
1 slice fresh ginger

Wash the fruits carefully. Peel and core the pears and pineapple, removing the eyes of the latter. Rough chop the lemon and orange, discarding the pips only. Put all the fruit through a grinder with a coarse blade, catching as much of the juice as possible. Put in a pot with the sugar; add the spices tied in a muslin bag. Bring to a boil, stirring until the sugar dissolves. Simmer for 30 minutes or until set.

Remove the spice bag and ladle into hot sterilized jars, leaving ¼-inch headspace. Wipe the rims clean, put the lids in place, and tighten down. Invert the jars for a few minutes, then return to the upright and let cool completely. Check the seals, label, and store in a cool, dry place.

Lychee Jam

Yield: about 3 cups

The texture of fresh lychees is very similar to the rubbery canned variety, but the fresh ones are very juicy and refreshing. The color of this jam is rosy and clear, its flavor...intriguing.

✂ INGREDIENTS ✂

2 pounds lychees
3¾ cups sugar
juice of 2 lemons

Peel the lychees, pop out the pits, and either grind or chop the flesh. Put the fruit in a saucepan with the sugar and the lemon juice. Bring slowly to a boil, stirring until the sugar dissolves; boil gently until the jam sets, about 20 minutes. Let cool slightly before potting to prevent floating fruit.

Ladle into hot sterilized jars, leaving ¼-inch headspace; if you notice a continued tendency of the fruit to float to the top, let cool further, then stir the contents of each jar with a spoon. Remove air bubbles with a nonmetallic spatula if necessary. Wipe the rims clean, put the lids in place, and tighten down. Invert the jars for a few minutes to complete the seal, then return to the upright and let cool completely. Check the seals, label, and store in a cool, dry place.

Strawberry-Pineapple Conserve

Yield: about 4½ cups

> ### ✄ INGREDIENTS ✄
>
> 1 pound strawberries
> half of 1 small pineapple
> 3 cups sugar

Wash, dry, and hull the strawberries. Peel, core, and finely chop, or, in a grinder, crush the pineapple; you should have about 1 cup of crushed fruit. Combine the pineapple and sugar in a pan, stirring until the sugar is dissolved. Simmer gently for 10 minutes; add the strawberries and continue to cook until thick and clear, another 20 minutes or so.

Put into hot sterilized jars, leaving ¼-inch headspace; stir a few times before sealing to prevent fruit floating to the top. Wipe the rims clean, put the lids in place, and tighten down. Invert the jars for a few minutes, then return to the upright and let cool completely. Check the seals, label, and store in a cool, dry place.

Sapote Jam

Yield: about 2 cups

This exotic fruit has a bright green paper-thin skin and creamy white, sweet pulp. The texture is refreshing, if slightly slimy. There is one largish pit, but there may also be additional undeveloped flat ones which will float free in the cooking. The jam is bright green, slightly granular, and mild but interesting in flavor.

> ### ✄ INGREDIENTS ✄
>
> 1 pound of sapotes, about 6
> juice of 1 lemon
> 2 cups sugar

Wash and cut up the fruit, removing the larger pits. Cover with the juice of 1 lemon and the sugar; let stand 3–4 hours, until juiced up. Put all in a pan, bring gently to a boil, and

SAPOTES

Kiwi Jam

Yield: about 4 cups

One of the kiwi's charms is its inner beauty: the cool green flesh punctuated with myriad black seeds. This refreshing jam retains that beauty, the seeds providing a fine textural counterpoint.

✂ INGREDIENTS ✂

2 pounds slightly underripe kiwis (8 or 9)
4 cups sugar

simmer until set, about 20 minutes. Let stand a few minutes to dissipate the foam; skim off any residue and any pits that have floated free.

Place into hot sterililized jars, leaving ¼-inch headspace. Wipe the rims clean, put the lids in place, and tighten down. Invert the jars for a few minutes, then return to the upright and let cool completely. Check the seals, label, and store in a cool, dry place.

Cut the kiwis in half and scoop the flesh out into a bowl. Pour the sugar over the fruit and let sit for 1 hour to juice up. Place all in a pot and bring gently to a boil, stirring until the sugar is dissolved. Boil for 15–20 minutes, until set. Cool slightly, stirring occasionally to discourage the fruit from floating to the top.

Ladle into hot sterilized jars, leaving ¼-inch headspace. Wipe the rims clean, put the lids in place, and tighten down. Invert the jars for a few minutes, then return to the upright and let cool completely. Check the seals, label, and store in a cool, dry place.

The Citrus Grove

Tangerine and Lime Marmalade

Yield: about 7 cups

Most marmalades require at least two steps: overnight soaking followed by a long cooking period. Some recipes require up to four separate steps. This one, however, offers an interesting combination of flavors as well as one-day preparation. The colors are sunny and the product worth the extra work of the fine-slicing, though the jelly is not as translucent as usual.

✗ INGREDIENTS ✗

9 tangerines

3 limes

5 cups water

6 cups sugar

Wash all the fruits and squeeze the juice, then slice the rinds as thin as possible. Put the juice and the rinds in a saucepan with the water, bring to a boil, and simmer until the rind is soft, about 1 hour. Add the sugar, stirring until dissolved, and continue to boil until set, about 20–30 minutes longer.

Ladle into hot sterilized jars, leaving ¼-inch headspace. Wipe the rims clean, put the lids in place, and tighten down. Invert the jars for a few minutes, then return to the upright and let cool completely. Check the seals, label, and store in a cool, dry place.

Tangerine Jelly

Yield: about 4 cups

✄ INGREDIENTS ✄

2 pounds tangerines

1 grapefruit

2 lemons

10 cups water

sugar: 1 cup per cup of juice
(you will need 5–6 cups for this recipe)

Wash and halve all the fruit; scoop the pulp out into a very large, heavy saucepan. Chop all the peels and add to the pan. Add the water, bring to a boil, and simmer until the peel is tender, about 2 hours.

When tender, strain through a jelly bag, taking care not to squeeze the bag. Measure the juice thus obtained, return it to the saucepan and add 1 cup of sugar for each cup of juice. Boil to set, about 20–30 minutes.

Skim off any foam and ladle into hot sterilized jars, leaving ¼-inch headspace. Wipe the rims clean, put the lids in place, and tighten down. Invert the jars for a few minutes, then return to the upright and let cool completely. Check the seals, label, and store in a cool, dry place.

TANGERINE JELLY

Three-Fruit Marmalade

Yield: about 5 cups

✂ INGREDIENTS ✂

1 grapefruit

2 oranges

1½ lemons

2½ quarts water

6 cups sugar

Wash the fruit and squeeze out the juice. Peel all the outer rinds, then chop or slice the rinds very fine. Put the piths and pips in a large muslin bag. Place the fruit juice, peels, and the muslin bag in a bowl with the water and let stand covered overnight.

In the morning, transfer the contents of the bowl to a very large pot, bring to a boil, and let simmer, uncovered, for about 2 hours.

Remove the muslin bag to a colander set in a bowl; when the bag is a little cooled, squeeze out any remaining juices and return the liquid to the pot. Stir the sugar into the fruit mixture until dissolved, then boil rapidly until set, about 30 minutes.

Ladle into hot sterilized jars, leaving ¼-inch headspace. Wipe the rims clean, put the lids in place, and tighten down. Invert the jars for a few minutes, then return to the upright and let cool completely. Check the seals, label, and store in a cool, dry place.

Grapefruit-Lemon Jelly

Yield: about 6 cups

This jelly, wonderful on its own, is also a terrific base for an herbal jelly—sage or tarragon, in particular. Add a small bundle of the fresh herb to the juice at the same time as the sugar; remove before potting.

✂ INGREDIENTS ✂

2 grapefruits (about 2 pounds)

2 lemons

6 cups water

sugar: 1 cup per cup of juice
(you will need 6–7 cups for this recipe)

Wash and peel all the fruit; roughly chop the pith and peel, then the flesh, taking care not to lose the juice, which is why you chop the flesh separately from the rind. Put the lot (fruit peel, juices, flesh, and pith) together with the water and the pips, in a pot, bring to a boil, and cook for 2 hours.

Strain through a jelly bag. Measure the juice obtained, place in a large saucepan and add 1 cup of sugar for each cup of juice, stirring until dissolved. Cook only 4 cups of juice at a time. Boil fast until set (5–10 minutes). Remove herbs if you have used them; skim as necessary.

Ladle the jelly into hot sterilized jars, leaving ¼-inch headspace. Wipe the rims clean, put the lids in place, and tighten down. Invert the jars for a few minutes, then return to the upright and let cool completely. Check the seals, label, and store in a cool, dry place.

Grapefruit Marmalade

Yield: about 4 cups

Choose yellow or red grapefruit depending on whether you want pinkish or golden marmalade. The Ruby Red variety will yield a less flavorful product.

✂ INGREDIENTS ✂

1 large grapefruit

1 lemon

5 cups water

4 cups sugar

Wash the grapefruit and lemon, grate the outer rinds (or peel and slice fine), and place in a bowl with 5 cups of water. Remove the pith and pips to a muslin bag; chop the pulp. Put all together in the bowl of water and let stand, covered, overnight.

In the morning, transfer the contents of the bowl to a large saucepan, bring to a boil and simmer, covered, until the rinds are tender, an hour or more. Remove the muslin bag into the pot and let it drain back into the saucepan. If you like a bitter marmalade, squeeze the bag into the pot to get all the juices out; without this squeezing, the marmalade will be quite mild. Stir in the sugar and boil rapidly to set, about 15 minutes.

Skim as necessary, then ladle into hot sterilized jars, leaving ¼-inch headspace. Wipe the rims clean, put the lids in place, and tighten down. Invert the jars for a few minutes, then return to the upright and let cool completely. Check the seals, label, and store in a cool, dry place.

Blood Orange Marmalade

Yield: about 6 cups

BLOOD ORANGE MARMALADE

✂ INGREDIENTS ✂

2 pounds blood oranges (6 or 7)

1 lemon

8 cups water

6–7 cups of sugar

Scrub the fruit, sliced or chopped fine according to your preference, and remove the pips to a muslin bag. Let stand in a bowl overnight with the pips and enough water to cover (about 8 cups).

In the morning, transfer all to a pan and bring to a boil, then simmer until the peel is soft and the contents reduced by half, about 2 hours. Measure the contents of the pan at this point and add 1 cup sugar for each cup of fruit, stirring until dissolved. Boil gently until set, about 40 minutes.

Cool slightly before ladling into hot sterilized jars, leaving ¼-inch headspace. Wipe the rims clean, put the lids in place, and tighten down. Invert the jars for a few minutes, then return to the upright and let cool completely. Check the seals, label, and store in a cool, dry place.

Lime Marmalade

Yield: about 3 cups

✂ INGREDIENTS ✂

4 limes (1 pound)

5 cups water

5 cups sugar

Wash the limes well. Slice very fine, discarding the end pieces with their pith. Put the pips, if any, in a muslin bag.

Put the fruit and the bag into a large bowl with the water and let stand, covered, overnight. In the morning, boil for 1½ hours or until the peel is tender. Do not undercook. Remove the bag of pips, bring the fruit back to a boil and add the sugar, stirring until dissolved. Boil rapidly until set, about 20 minutes.

As the prolonged cooking tends to destroy the color, you may wish to add green food coloring, one drop at a time, until the desired color is achieved. Stir in well.

Ladle marmalade into hot sterilized jars, leaving ¼-inch headspace. Wipe the rims clean, put the lids in place, and tighten down. Invert the jars for a few minutes, then return to the upright and let cool completely. Check the seals, label, and store in a cool, dry place.

Lemon Jelly

Yield: about 4½ cups

✂ INGREDIENTS ✂

6 lemons (about 1¼ pounds)
sugar: (you will need 4–5 cups for this recipe)
1 cup per cup of juice)

Wash the fruit well, cut into quarters horizontally; remove and discard the pips and the end pieces with their pith. Put in a

large bowl with a generous amount of water to cover and let stand overnight.

In the morning, boil, covered, for 2 hours, then strain through a jelly bag. Measure the juice obtained and put it in a pan with 1 cup of sugar for each cup of juice, stirring until the sugar dissolves. Boil until set, another 15 minutes or so.

Ladle into hot sterilized jars, leaving ¼-inch headspace. Wipe the rims clean, put the lids in place, and tighten down. Invert the jars for a few minutes, then return to the upright and let cool completely. Check the seals, label, and store in a cool, dry place.

Lemon Curd

Yield: about 4½ cups

Careful storage is crucial to the safe keeping of this spread. The year-round availability of the ingredients means that it can be made in small batches as needed. Do not try to keep it for more than two or three months. Lemon curd is delicious as a filler for tiny tartlets or layer cakes, on toast or bread, or even with peanut butter in a sandwich.

⚜ INGREDIENTS ⚜

2 lemons

½ cup butter

6 eggs, well-beaten

Wash the lemons and grate the outer rinds very fine, avoiding the bitter pith; squeeze the juice and strain. Place the rind, juice, sugar, and butter in the top of a double boiler over, but not in, simmering water. Cook and stir until the butter melts and the sugar is dissolved. Remove from the heat. Stir a little of the hot mixture into the well-beaten eggs, then stir the eggs back into the rest of the mixture in the top of the double boiler. Return the double boiler to the heat. Continue to cook, stirring constantly, until thick, about 10 minutes.

Ladle into hot, sterilized jars, leaving ¼-inch headspace. Shake firmly to eliminate air bubbles. Wipe the rims clean, put the lids in place, and tighten down, but do not invert the bottles. Let cool completely; check the seals, label, and store in a cool, dry place.

LEMON CURD MAKES AN EXCELLENT FILLING FOR A DESSERT TART.

Something from the Bar

Pearnod Preserve

Yield: about 4½ cups

Pears, subtle themselves, are a perfect vehicle for the anise flavor of Pernod, but are easily overwhelmed, too. Add the Pernod very gradually, off the heat, at the end of the cooking. A very little goes a long way; the right combination is exquisite.

PEARNOD PRESERVE

✄ INGREDIENTS ✄

6 pears, ripe but firm

3 apples

juice of 1½ lemons

3¾ cups sugar

2 or 3 tablespoons Pernod

Wash, peel, core, and quarter the pears and apples, then cut the quarters into small pieces. Tie the peels in a muslin bag. Place the fruit and the muslin bag in a saucepan with a minimal amount of water; cover and cook until the fruit is quite pulpy, about 20 minutes. Remove the muslin bag; add the lemon juice and then add the sugar gradually, stirring until completely dissolved. Return to a boil and cook briskly at first, stirring occasionally.

As the pears cook down and approach setting, you will need to stir almost constantly over low heat to prevent scorching; this may take as long as 30 minutes. When set, remove from the heat and add the Pernod, a tablespoon at a time, until the flavor is satisfactory.

Ladle the preserves into hot sterilized jars, leaving ¼-inch headspace. Wipe the rims clean, put the lids in place, and

tighten down. Invert the jars for a few minutes, then return to the upright. Shake firmly to eliminate any trapped air bubbles. Let cool completely. Check the seals, label, and store in a cool, dry place.

Chardonnay Jelly with Passion Fruit

Yield: about 5 cups

✄ INGREDIENTS ✄

8 passion fruit

1 cup water

2 cups Chardonnay wine

1 tablespoon lemon juice

3 tablespoons powdered pectin

4 cups sugar

Halve the passion fruit and scoop out the pulp and seeds; place in a saucepan with the water and simmer gently for 10 minutes. Put through a sieve, forcing the pulp off the seeds with a wooden spoon. Place this juice in a large saucepan with the wine, the lemon juice, and the pectin. Bring to a boil, stirring constantly. As soon as a rolling boil is reached, add the sugar;

return to a boil, stirring constantly. Remove from the heat, as soon as a rolling boil is reached. Skim.

Ladle into hot sterilized jars, leaving ¼-inch headspace. Wipe the rims clean, put the lids in place, and tighten down. Invert the jars for a few minutes, then return to the upright and let cool completely. Check the seals, label, and store in a cool, dry place.

May Wine Jelly

Yield: about 4½ cups

Sweet woodruff is not readily available at your local produce stand, but it flourishes as a ground cover in shady places in the backyard. It is carefree and hardy, yet of delicate appearance. Its apple green leafage darkens as the season advances. The jelly is light and pleasant, but not redolent of its herbal content, since woodruff itself has a subtle flavor.

✂ INGREDIENTS ✂

2 cups Moselle or other soft
German white wine

10 sprigs young sweet woodruff

2 tablespoons lemon juice

2 tablespoons powdered pectin

3 cups sugar

Put the wine and the sweet woodruff in a saucepan and let stand 20 minutes, no longer. Stir in the lemon juice and the powdered pectin. Bring to a boil and add the sugar, stirring until completely dissolved. Return to a rolling boil; as soon as this occurs, remove from the heat and skim off the foam, at the same time removing the sweet woodruff.

Pour into hot sterilized jars, leaving ¼-inch headspace. Wipe the rims clean, put the lids in place, and tighten down. Invert the jars for a few minutes to complete the seal, then return to the upright and let cool completely. Check the seals, label, and store in a cool, dry place.

Margarita Jelly

Yield: about 5 cups

Ascertain whether you really like Tequila before attempting this interesting jelly. If you are a Margarita fan, then you will recognize and enjoy the taste of this jellied version of the cocktail on your toast in the morning or in the afternoon on crackers, served with aperitifs.

✂ INGREDIENTS ✂

1½ cups water

3 cups sugar

rind of 1 lime

3 tablespoons powdered pectin

1 cup tequila

¼ cup Triple Sec

½ cup lime juice (4–6 limes)

Put the water and sugar in a large, deep saucepan with the outer rind (no pith) of 1 lime, cut into long strips. Sprinkle the powdered pectin over the surface, then stir constantly until it dissolves and the syrup comes to an exuberant boil. Boil for 5 minutes. Add the tequila, Triple Sec, and lime juice; stir, bring back to a full boil, and remove from the heat.

Skim and pour into hot sterilized jars, leaving ¼-inch headspace. Add one strip of lime peel to each jar. Wipe the rims clean, put the lids in place, and tighten down. Invert the jars for a few minutes to complete the seal, then return to the upright and let cool completely. Check the seals, label, and store in a cool, dry place.

Kir Jelly

Yield: about 4 cups

✄ INGREDIENTS ✄

2 cups white wine

¼ cup creme de cassis

¾ cup water

4 strips lemon rind (no pith)

¼ cup lemon juice

3 tablespoons powdered pectin

4 cups sugar

Mix together in a large, deep pot the white wine, creme de cassis, water, lemon rind, and lemon juice. Sprinkle the powdered pectin over the surface and stir until dissolved. Bring to a rolling boil, stirring constantly. Add the sugar at once, stirring until dissolved. Return to a boil, then remove from the heat at once.

Skim and pour into hot sterilized jars, leaving ¼-inch headspace. Place one strip of lemon peel in each jar. Wipe the rims clean, put the lids in place, and tighten down. Invert the jars for a few minutes to vacuum seal, then return to the upright and let cool completely. Check the seals, label, and store in a cool, dry place.

Sangria Jelly

Yield: about 4 cups

✄ INGREDIENTS ✄

¼ cup orange juice

2 tablespoons lemon juice

1½ cups Burgundy wine

2 tablespoons Cointreau

3 cups sugar

3-ounce pouch liquid pectin

Stir the fruit juices, wine, and Cointreau together in the top of a double boiler. Place over, but not in, boiling water, and add the sugar. Stir until the sugar is completely dissolved and the mixture piping hot. Remove from the heat and immediately add the pectin, stirring in well.

Skim off the foam and pour into hot sterilized jars, leaving ¼-inch headspace. Wipe the rims clean, put the lids in place, and tighten down. Invert the jars for a few minutes to complete the seal, then return to the upright and let cool completely. Check the seals, label, and store in a cool, dry place.

SANGRIA JELLY

Negus Jelly (Mulled Wine)

Yield: about 6 cups

✂ INGREDIENTS ✂

1½ cups water

4 cups sugar

6 cloves

1 cinnamon stick

pinch of ground nutmeg

½ lemon

½ orange

½ cup lime juice

2 cups Burgundy wine

6 ounces liquid pectin

Make the syrup by placing the water, sugar, and spices in a large, deep saucepan. Remove the peels from the lemon and the orange with a vegetable peeler; add the peels to the syrup. Bring to a boil, stirring until the sugar is dissolved, then let boil rapidly for 5 minutes. Remove from the heat, add ½ cup lime juice, strain, and return to the pot. Set aside a few long pieces of the citrus peel.

Add 2 cups of Burgundy wine to the syrup; return to a full boil and immediately add the liquid pectin. Return to a boil and remove from the heat at once.

Pour into hot sterilized jars, leaving ¼-inch headspace. Add one piece of the citrus peel used in making the syrup to each jar of jelly (optional). Wipe the rims of the jars clean, put the lids in place and tighten down. Invert the jars for a few minutes to vacuum seal, then return to the upright and let cool completely. The jelly may take a day or two to set properly—be patient. Check the seals, label, and store in a cool, dry place.

NEGUS JELLY

Preserves for Dessert

Peaches in Bordeaux

Yield: about 1 quart

✂ INGREDIENTS ✂

½ cup raspberries, fresh or frozen whole

¾ cup Bordeaux wine (or Merlot or Cabernet Sauvignon)

½ cup water

½ cup sugar

2–3 pounds peaches

juice of 1 lemon

If using fresh berries, pick over and gently rinse.

Simmer the wine, water, and berries together until soft, then crush the berries. Sieve to remove the seeds. Return to the saucepan, add the sugar, stirring until dissolved, and bring to a boil. Set aside.

Scald the peaches, then plunge in cold water and slip off their skins. Halve, and remove the pits. Toss the peaches in a bowl with the lemon juice, then pack in hot sterilized jars. Bring the syrup back to a boil and pour over the peaches to within ½ inch of the rim. Use a nonmetallic spatula to eliminate air bubbles. Wipe the rims clean, put the lids in place, and tighten down. Process in a boiling water bath for 25 minutes; remove, invert for a few minutes, return to the upright, and let cool completely. Check the seals, label, and store in a cool, dry place.

Clementines in Cointreau

Yield: about 3 pints

> ## ✗ INGREDIENTS ✗
>
> 2 pounds Clementines
>
> 1 orange
>
> 1 cup sugar
>
> 1 stick cinnamon
>
> 2–3 cloves
>
> 3 cups water
>
> ½ cup Cointreau or Grand Marnier

Peel the Clementines and remove as many of the white fibers as possible. Carefully separate the segments. Slice the unpeeled orange and put it in a pot with the Clementines; add water to cover. Bring to a boil; simmer for 15 minutes. Remove all of the fruit, discarding the orange slices. Set the Clementine segments aside.

Measure the 3 cups of liquid in the pan; add 1 cup of sugar, the cinnamon, and the cloves. Boil for 5 minutes, then remove the cinnamon stick and return the Clementines to the pot. Simmer 10 minutes. Remove from the heat; gently stir in ½ cup of Cointreau or Grand Marnier.

Ladle the fruit into hot sterilized jars and top up with syrup, leaving ¼-inch headspace. Wipe the rims clean, put the lids in place, and tighten down. Process in a water bath for 20 minutes. Remove the jars from the water bath and invert for 10 minutes, then return to the upright, shaking firmly to eliminate air bubbles. Let cool completely. Check the seals, label, and store in a cool, dry place.

Candied Preserved Kumquats

Yield: about 1 pound

> ## ✗ INGREDIENTS ✗
>
> 1 pound kumquats
>
> 3½ cups sugar
>
> 6 cups water
>
> cream of tartar

Wash kumquats well in warm soapy water; rinse well and remove all stem ends. Cover with fresh water. Bring slowly to a boil and cook for 15 minutes. Drain through a colander and repeat the process twice, using fresh water and discarding it after each boiling. This process helps remove the bitterness of the skins.

Make a syrup using 1½ cups of the sugar and 4 cups of the water; boil 5 minutes before adding the drained kumquats. Bring back to the boil and cook until the fruit is translucent. Remove the kumquats from the syrup and drain.

Make another syrup using 2 cups of sugar, 2 cups of water, and a pinch of cream of tartar. Put the kumquats in this syrup and boil for 30 minutes. Remove from the heat and let stand in the syrup for 24 hours.

Bring to a boil the next day and cook again for 30 minutes. Drain once more and dry the kumquats on a rack. Roll in granulated sugar. Store in an airtight container.

Kumquat Preserve

Yield: about 3 cups

✂ INGREDIENTS ✂

3 pounds kumquats

per cup of liquid:

1 cup sugar

¼ cup honey

KUMQUAT PRESERVE MAKES A DELICIOUS TOPPING FOR VANILLA ICE CREAM.

Wash fruit with warm, soapy water and rinse well. Without peeling, slice the fruit and remove the pips. Put the fruit in a pan with enough water to cover. Bring to a boil and simmer 15 minutes. Drain into a bowl; set the kumquats aside and measure the liquid. For each cup of liquid, add 1 cup of sugar and ¼ cup of honey. Return to heat and bring this syrup to a boil; simmer 5 minutes. Return the drained fruit to the syrup and continue to cook until the fruit is transparent, about 45 minutes.

Carefully ladle the fruit into hot sterilized jars, then continue to cook the syrup until thick. Pour the syrup over the fruit in the jars, leaving ¼-inch headspace. Use a nonmetallic spatula to eliminate air bubbles. Wipe the rims clean, put the lids in place, and tighten down. Invert the jars for a few minutes, then return to the upright, shake firmly to eliminate air bubbles, and let cool completely. Check the seals, label, and store in a cool, dry place.

Margarita Pears

Yield: about 3 pints

⚔ INGREDIENTS ⚔

6 Asian pears

1 lime

1½ cups water

½ cup Tequila

1 cup sugar

With a slotted spoon, remove the pears from the syrup. Pack the pears two to a hot sterilized pint jar, with one strip of lime in each jar. Pour the hot syrup over the pears, leaving ¼-inch headspace. Wipe the rims clean, put the lids in place, and tighten down. Process for 20 minutes in a boiling water bath; remove and invert for a few minutes, then return to the upright and let cool completely. Check the seals, label, and store in a cool, dry place.

MARGARITA PEARS

Brandied Pineapple

Yield: about 3 cups

INGREDIENTS

1 large pineapple
½ cup sugar
1 stick cinnamon
2–3 cloves
½ cup brandy

Peel and core the pineapple; remove the eyes. Cut into bite-sized chunks and weigh out 2 pounds. Put in a pan with water just to cover (about 1½ cups). Simmer until the pineapple is tender; remove the fruit from the syrup with a slotted spoon and set aside. Stir in the sugar and spices; boil until syrupy. Remove from the heat and add ½ cup brandy. Remove the cinnamon stick, but leave the cloves if you wish.

Pack the pineapple in hot sterilized jars. Pour the syrup over the fruit, leaving ¼-inch headspace. Make sure no air bubbles remain. Wipe the rims, put the lids in place, and tighten down. Process in a hot water bath for 10 minutes. Remove from the water bath and let cool completely. Check the seals, label, and store in a cool, dry place.

BRANDIED PINEAPPLE

Alltrista
P.O. Box 2005
Muncie, IN 47307-0005
(800) 428-8150
Ball and Kerr products

Aphrodisia
264 Bleecker Street
New York, NY 10014
(212) 989-6440
Dried herbs and spices, vanilla beans

Balducci's
424 Avenue of the Americas
New York, NY 10011
(800) 225-3822
Fine exotic fruits and vegetables shipped anywhere in the United States

Broadway Panhandler
477 Broom St.
New York, NY 10012
(212) 966-3434
Mason jars, spice jars, fine cooking equipment

Chef's Catalog
3215 Commercial Avenue
Northbrook, IL 60062-1600
(800) 338-3232
Decorative vinegar bottles, tins, jars, decorative bottle stoppers, and cooking equipment

The Crate and Barrel
P.O. Box 9059
Wheeling, IL 60090-9059
(800) 323-5461
Various housewares, jars

Frieda's, Inc.
4465 Corporate Center Drive
Los Alamitos, CA 90720-2561
(714) 826-6100
Huge variety of fine exotic fruits and vegetables shipped anywhere in the United States

Gardener's Supply Company
128 Intervale Road
Burlington, VT 05401
(802) 863-1700
fax (802) 660-4600
Canning equipment

Glashaus, Inc.
415 W. Golf Road, Ste. 13
Arlington Heights, IL 60005
(847) 640-6910
Rubber rings

Hold Everything
P.O. Box 7807
San Francisco, CA 94120
(800) 421-2264
fax (415) 421-5153
Decorative seasonal tins, boxes, and baskets

Kitchen Krafts
P.O. Box 442
Waukon, IA 52172
(800) 776-4960
Food preservation equipment, kitchen labels and supplies

Merex Inc.
1120 Saw Mill River Road
Yonkers, NY 10710-0009
(914) 376-0202
(800) 513-3335
Huge variety of fine exotic fruits and vegetables shipped anywhere in the United States

Milan Laboratories
57 Spring Street
New York, NY 10012
(212) 226-4780
Vinegar-making kits, bottles, and bottling equipment

Rafal Spice Co.
2521 Russell Street
Detroit, MI 48207
(800) 228-4276
Pickling spices, herbs

Sears, Roebuck and Co.
Telecatalog Center
9390 Bunsen Parkway
Louisville, KY 40220
(800) 366-3125
Pressure canners

Victorian Papers
P.O. Box 411332
Dept. CH 893
Kansas City, MO 64141
(800) 800-6647
Lovely Victorian labels and gift bags

William Glen
Mail-Order Department
2651 El Paseo Lane
Sacramento, CA 95821
(800) 842-3322
Fine cooking equipment

Williams-Sonoma
Mail-Order Department
P.O. Box 7456
San Francisco, CA 94120
(800) 541-2233
Fine cooking equipment

Woodtown Specialties
360 E. 55th Street, Rm. 6G
New York, NY 10022
(212) 371-4919
Attractive, coordinated labels; decorative gift packaging; kits for canned goods; recipe cards; decorative fabric tops and bottle bags

Zabar's
2245 Broadway
New York, NY 10024
(212) 787-2000
Widemouth pint jars, 1/2-gallon widemouth jars; fine exotic fruits and vegetables shipped anywhere in the United States